Praise for *The Hero is You*

"The goal of certified life coach Levin's book
developing a deeper understanding of story
archetypes that make up a hero's journey, an
will help them feel more in tune with them
guides readers through the labyrinth of the
as the "hero's journey"—a quest for identity and wholeness. Guidelines
require writers to ask questions, explore their vulnerabilities, and seek
mentors. Exercises and quizzes move authors toward self-examination.
VERDICT: This guide would serve as a valuable text for writers' groups or
beginning classes on the craft."

—Deborah Bigelow, *Library Journal*

"The title says it all. Every writer faces a journey that wends through a
nettlesome labyrinth of challenges and obstacles. It takes a hero to leap
into the uncertain terrain of a new creative venture, conquer self-doubt,
and persist across the craggy lands found in all creative projects. Kendra
Levin's wise, encouraging words provide guidance every step of the way to
help every writer realize their creative goals."

—Grant Faulkner, executive director of National Novel
Writing Month and co-founder of *100 Word Story*

"With the perfect combination of encouragement and practical advice,
Kendra Levin inspires writers of every stripe in *The Hero Is You*. Acting
as the coach by your side, she helps unlock your true talent, conquer your
fears, and write your best work. If you want to take your writing to the
next level, buy this book . . . now!"

—Arielle Eckstut and David Henry Sterry, The Book Doctors and
authors of *The Essential Guide to Getting Your Book Published*

"If I were to name the one quality that writers need in order to get their
books written, it would be courage. Kendra Levin knows all about this
necessary heroism and helps writers step to the plate in this much-needed
guide to the brave writing life."

—Eric Maisel, author of *Coaching the Artist Within*

"Smart, perceptive, and inspirational advice from an encouraging
book editor."

—Susan Shapiro, *New York Times* best-selling author of
Unhooked and *Only as Good as Your Word*

the

hero

is

you

the hero is you

SHARPEN YOUR FOCUS, CONQUER YOUR DEMONS, AND
BECOME THE WRITER YOU WERE BORN TO BE

KENDRA LEVIN
Certified Life Coach

Conari Press

An OPEN CENTER Book™

This edition first published in 2016 by Conari Press, an imprint of
Red Wheel/Weiser, LLC

With offices at:
65 Parker Street, Suite 7
Newburyport, MA 01950
www.redwheelweiser.com

ISBN: 978-1-57324-688-0

Library of Congress Cataloging-in-Publication Data available upon request.

Cover design by Cara Petrus
Cover art © aleksandarvelasevic / Getty Images
Interior images by Jim Hoover
Interior design by Debby Dutton
Typeset in Adobe Caslon text and Avenir and Book Antiqua display

Printed in the United States of America
M&G
10 9 8 7 6 5 4 3 2 1

For my parents, with love and gratitude,
and with special thanks to Andrea Adams,
who sparked the idea and much more.

contents

introduction

We have not even to risk the adventure alone; for the heroes of all time have gone before us; the labyrinth is thoroughly known; we have only to follow the thread of the hero-path. And where we had thought to find an abomination, we shall find a god; where we had thought to slay another, we shall slay ourselves; where we had thought to travel outward, we shall come to the center of our own existence; where we had thought to be alone, we shall be with all the world.

—Joseph Campbell, *The Hero with a Thousand Faces*

It's a Tuesday morning and a writer comes to me with a problem.

I just don't feel on top of my game, she writes in an email. *And I need to be, for a thousand reasons. Do you know what I mean?*

I do, and all too well. Just the day before, I was struggling through what felt like a terrible draft of the book you're holding and couldn't seem to get myself to a good place with it. As an editor and life coach for writers, I'm used to supporting writers, asking them questions, and challenging them to find their way out of quagmires. What I'm *not* used to is being in a quagmire myself.

I'm crafting my response to her when I get a phone call from Lindsey, one of the authors I edit. She wants to talk through a story issue in the novel she's writing, but it quickly becomes clear she's dealing with more than simply a plot problem. Her confidence is at an all-time low.

"I know I've done this before," she says. "But this time, I don't think I'm going to make it to the other side."

This is her third published novel, the fifth or sixth she's written. It's heartbreaking to see her struggle like this, yet I can't help but be inspired by the fact that she's fought her way through the peaks and valleys of this difficult process that many times—and emerged from it with books she was proud of.

"Remember when you said that last time?" I ask her. "And the time before that? What helped you get through those rough patches then?"

By the time we hang up, she sounds calmer and has promised she'll go for a walk to clear her head. She's also managed to generate some options to solve her story issue.

After my workday at Penguin ends, I see coaching clients. Rosalita is struggling with discipline; she sought my help after spending several years nibbling at her memoir, making only incremental progress. "The night before, I always say, 'Tomorrow, I'm going to write for four hours,'" she tells me. "But then I get up, and when I turn on my phone, I've got a text from my friend, so I text her back . . . and then while I'm waiting for her to respond, I look at my email and Facebook . . . and the next thing I know, the whole morning's gone."

"Do other writers go through this?" she asks me. I want to tell her I've been going through it myself. Instead, I just say, "Of course."

The Creative Labyrinth

What do *you* most struggle with in your writing process? Do you find it difficult to work when you're just not "in the mood"? Do you get hung up in the middle of a project like Lindsey, hitting a wall and panicking? Do you have a hard time resisting distractions and getting your butt in the chair, like Rosalita?

Or maybe you're not like any of these writers. Maybe what you've struggled with is finding ideas or getting started—or knowing when the piece is finished. Maybe when you're faced with a decision in your work, you have a hard time knowing which route to take. Perhaps you struggle with asking other people to help and support you in your process. You might be most confounded by trying to see your writing objectively or from a different perspective. It might be that you work so hard, you lose your sense of fun and play and writing becomes drudgery. Or what gives you the hardest time could be taking things you've learned and applying them to your work.

For more than a decade, I've worked with writers as an editor, teacher, and life coach. I've helped people writing fiction and nonfiction for both adults and young readers—many working on novels, but also poetry, screenplays, plays, picture books, articles, memoirs, blogs, and even puppet shows. Actors, dancers, and choreographers have also come to me for aid with finding a healthy balance between life and art.

I know firsthand how hard it is to find that balance. For many years, I wrote fiction and plays, and my work was produced Off-Broadway when I was twenty. I won awards and had articles written about me. Then I freaked out, "quit" writing, and spent several years cut off from being creative—and several more writing in secret after that. Crises of confidence, paralysis on the page, navigating the perilous waters of getting published—I've seen it, I've lived it, and I've helped other writers get through it.

No matter who you are or how long you've been making your art, the creative process can feel like a labyrinth. Each time you start a new piece of work, it's hard to know what twists and turns lie ahead, or to be prepared for what you'll learn and how you'll evolve by the time you come out the other side. When something obstructs the path, we often can't help but throw up our hands and ask ourselves, *Will I ever get past this?*

You can and you will. I'm here to show you how.

Focusing on Process

A writer friend told me about seeing J. K. Rowling speak and having the chance to put in a question for the Harry Potter author to answer onstage. When I asked if she submitted one, she said no. "There's only one question I want to ask J. K. Rowling," she said, "and it's one she can't answer: *How did you do it?*"

When we ask the writers we admire about their writing schedules, or their processes, or what their favorite cereal is to eat and what time they like to eat it at, what we're really asking is, *How can I do what you do, the way you do it?*

But here's a more important question: *How can I do what I do in the way that will help me do my best work?*

Most books about writing either promise to extract a full manuscript from you in a specific time frame or instruct you, topic by topic, on areas of craft. There are many wonderful books like this out there; you'll see some of my favorites quoted throughout these pages and listed in the bibliography.

But many books and writing programs place so much emphasis on craft, they neglect one of the most challenging aspects of writing: how to go about actually getting the words from your brain onto the page on a regular basis. We ask admired writers *How did you do it?* because although there is no one right way to do it, we may have tried many ways that haven't worked for us.

What I always yearned for as a writer, and never found, was a book that would help me establish a healthy, regular writing practice that was customized for me and would keep me writing, no matter what project I was working on at the time. Process is thorny to address in a book, because it's so incredibly personal to each individual writer. But being conscious about it is the most effective way to accomplish your goals. "Research shows that people who focus on the *process* of achieving a desired outcome are more likely to achieve it than those who simply think about the outcome itself," says psychologist Timothy D. Wilson.

In my years of working with artists, I've always wanted to pool the knowledge that all these brilliant, driven, courageous people have gleaned from their adventures in making art. You'll see some of these writers sharing their stories in this book, from bestselling and award-winning novelists to the writers of beloved television shows to stand-up comedians. You'll also hear the stories of my coaching clients—writers at varying levels of experience and external success—navigating the process, though their identifying details have been changed and some combined into composites to protect their privacy.

What stage of the writing process are *you* in right now?

Are you at the beginning of a new project, hoping to use this book to guide your process from step one? Are you struggling in the middle of a piece and wanting this book to lead you out of the woods? Or are you in a dry spell, seeking a source of inspiration to get you started on something new?

I want to share a tool with you that has helped guide the writers I've worked with through their own personal labyrinths.

The Hero's Journey

In the summer of 2010, I was sitting in a coffee shop with my friend Andrea doing what I usually do in a coffee shop: struggling to write. I'd promised to pen a blog post for an online writers' conference—something inspiring and motivating—and had left it until the very last minute. So naturally, I was mostly spending the time chatting with my friend.

Andrea was telling me about a course she was teaching on the Hero's Journey. I was familiar with the concept—that many stories follow a particular, fairly universal plot arc, with a character who overcomes a series of obstacles before encountering some big bad, emerging victorious, and going on to the next adventure—but that was about it. It struck me as we talked that being a writer working on a project is a lot like being a hero on a journey. Both have to face challenges of various kinds; both pick up lessons and tools along the way that they end up using; both emerge with a precious boon.

Andrea told me enough about the Hero's Journey that I could write five hundred words for the blog post, but I wanted to learn more. So I read the defining work on the subject, *The Hero with a Thousand Faces* by comparative mythology scholar Joseph Campbell. The 1949 book explores how this structure of storytelling has appeared in tales all over the world for thousands of years, from the first written legends to the latest films (which continues to be the case, since 1949's movies aren't exactly the most current). Such stories are populated by certain character types, or "archetypes," like the Mentor (wise older person who gives the Hero advice), the Trickster (character who is wily and cunning), and the Shadow (someone who represents evil, who works in opposition to whatever the Hero wants). Campbell drew inspiration for these archetypes from the work of psychologist Carl Jung, who coined the term "archetype" to mean a model for a behavior, person, or idea—a kind of lens through which to filter our experiences to explain them to ourselves.

Books like *The Writer's Journey*, which explains how to apply Campbell's ideas to screenwriting, and *The Heroine's Journey*, which looks at this mythic structure from more female-guided point of view, explore the subject further.

Many psychologists and writing teachers have used the Hero's Journey as a tool for psychotherapeutic work and writing craft. So I decided to start incorporating it into my work with my life coaching clients. I had a hunch it was a tool that would resonate with the writers I work with.

I was right. Whether they were plumbing the depths of their psyches on a guided visualization, using tools like the ones you'll find in this book to map goals and create structure in their processes, or recognizing difficult periods in writing and life as temporary stages of a long and fruitful journey, these writers relished the chance to see themselves as Heroes and to draw newfound inspiration from this age-old source. The Hero's Journey became a tool that helped them do some of their best work, find methods of structuring their time that kept them writing regularly, and be happier, more fulfilled people.

In this book, we'll look at Campbell's eight archetypes—Hero, Herald, Ally, Mentor, Threshold Guardian, Shapeshifter, Trickster, and Shadow—as well as a few I've added or embellished: Goddess, Superhero, Steed, and Mentor-Hero. In each chapter, we'll explore an archetype and see how we can use it as a metaphor for an aspect of the writing process and life. The Herald, for example, a character who shows up early in stories to summon the Hero to go on an adventure, can represent, for writers, getting new ideas, getting inspired, and beginning new projects. Each of these twelve characters holds the key to unlocking some aspect of your process where you may be stuck.

How to Use This Book

You might have come to this book with one or more specific projects in mind that you want to apply these ideas to, or you may just be reading it for general help. You can use it when you're starting a new piece, or to provide a jump-start if you stall out in the middle of one. You might read it all at once or dip in and out of it.

Before you begin, I recommend you get a new journal or blank book. In the chapters ahead, you'll find a raft of exercises that I'll be inviting you to do, and they're best done by hand on blank, nonruled paper. Of course, if working on a computer feels more natural to you, do that. I recommend doing exercises by hand because it's a more organic way of working and keeps you away from the tempting distractions that usually live on the computer, like email and the Internet, but do what works best for you.

Writing is often a solitary, isolating act, but being a writer doesn't have to be, and often benefits from company. The program in this book can be undertaken solo, but I encourage you to make it social. You might read the book with your critique group, a circle of writer friends, or even a collection of strangers that you bring together for this purpose. Or you might make an agreement with a writer friend or colleague to walk the steps of your Hero's Journey together.

Don't be surprised if you find yourself returning to the chapters, images, and exercises again. Though the story structure of the Hero's Journey has a beginning, middle, and end, the writer's journey never ends and isn't always linear. You may experience the stages of the journey in a totally different order than what's outlined here. You could go through a macro version over the course of your entire career or a micro version during a single writing session.

Naturally, there may be some aspects of this book that don't resonate with you at all, or that do, but only when inverted, turned inside out, or reinterpreted. This book is not a blueprint or formula; it's a jumping-off point. The only way to discover what works for you is by trying, and I encourage you to create your own variations and interpretations of the archetypes and exercises.

The Ball of String

Campbell wrote of the journey, "It is indeed very little that we need! But lacking that, the adventure into the labyrinth is without hope." Like the writers I've worked with and known—like a Hero—you already possess the talent, capability, and drive to write. Something in you *knows* it's time to make a change, whether it's a change to the structure of your piece, your approach to how you're writing, or your life. You heard a voice telling you to try something new, and you listened—you picked up this book.

In a later work, *The Power of Myth*, Campbell talks about how Ariadne gave the hero Theseus a ball of string to take into the labyrinth with him when he went to slay the Minotaur. The labyrinth was complicated, the monster was terrifying, and no one had ever escaped alive—but Theseus did. "All he had was the string," said Campbell. "That's all you need."

You're the Hero. The ball of string is in your hands. The rest is up to you.

CHAPTER ONE

the hero

identify your gifts and vulnerabilities and begin the work

You are already a **Hero**—whether you recognize it or not.

When I introduce the idea of the Hero's Journey as a metaphor for the writing process to the writers I work with, some inevitably balk. "I can't call myself a 'hero,'" one said to me early in our coaching relationship, "I haven't even done anything yet!"

But being a Hero doesn't mean you've rescued kittens from a tree or performed some feat of epic strength. By the time you reach the end of this chapter, you will have taken Heroic action. In fact, I'm willing to bet you've done so already without even realizing it.

When I met Lucy at a writers' conference, she was in the middle of a major transition in her life. At lunch, elbow-to-elbow in a packed hotel ballroom, she told me her story: she'd spent two decades climbing to the top of the heap of academia and had become a distinguished professor of computer science, paving the way for other women in a male-dominated field. But the work, which had never been her passion, seemed to grow more and more political. As she watched her daughter turn from toddler to child, she felt strongly that she wanted her daughter to grow up with a mother who pursued her dreams instead of one who complained bitterly about her work every night.

When we met, she was just about to get her masters degree in creative writing that she'd been pursuing on the side in a low-residency program. Her instructors had been encouraging, and friends she'd met through the program had even connected her with potential opportunities to earn money related to writing; freelance editing gigs, copywriting, and a chance to teach had all fallen into her lap with apparent serendipity. She could technically afford to walk away from her old career. But, she confided, she wasn't sure she was ready.

"Who am I if I'm not my job?" she asked as we finished our brownies. "After all these years and all this work, can 'writer' suddenly be who I am, like flipping a switch?"

"It sounds to me like 'writer' is already who you are," I told her, "whether you're ready to embrace that or not."

Six months later, I got an email from Lucy through my coaching website. She'd tracked me down to see if I was available to work with her, and I was delighted to get to hear the next chapter of her story.

She'd completed her degree, said yes to the opportunities that had come along, and was phasing out of her job. In her email, she described her anxiety, but on our first call, she was flush with excitement. In her new work, she was getting to tap into skills she'd known she had but never had the chance to use in her former life. And she was thrilled to be writing more.

A Hero, first and foremost, is a person on a quest for identity and wholeness.

"I still don't know who exactly I am," she told me cheerfully, "but I'm looking forward to finding out."

On the bumpy, confusing, ever-evolving journey toward being someone she could take pride in, Lucy was discovering what it means to be a Hero.

A Hero, first and foremost, is a person on a quest for identity and wholeness.

A Hero, first and foremost, is a person on a quest for identity and wholeness. Who am I? What is my place in the world? What am I on this earth to do? How do I find the places, the people, and the vocations that will fill me with satisfaction and fulfillment?

When you pursue the answers to these questions by seeking out change and by challenging yourself, you become a Hero.

Every writer is on a lifelong quest. When you have a passion for writing that compels you to create, you live in a constant state of rigorous exploration. Each project brings a new adventure, and a new opportunity to push your boundaries and discover hidden layers of riches inside you. **A Hero is a person with the potential for evolution.**

Another objection I've heard from writers reluctant to call themselves Heroes: "It sounds too self-important."

I'm not encouraging you to have an inflated ego. In fact, by acknowledging yourself as a Hero, you recognize that you are someone who still has lots to learn, who has the potential to grow into a more advanced version of yourself. You're at the beginning of a journey that will bring you face-to-face with your most frustrating weaknesses and flaws, push you to the limits of what you're capable of, and show you what's missing from your arsenal of skills. Being a Hero means that, instead of being cowed by these situations, you'll embrace the chance to strengthen those weaknesses, push those limits, and develop those skills.

To go on that quest for identity and wholeness, to bring about that evolution, you will have to step forward into change , like Lucy did. **A Hero is a person who says yes to the adventure.**

The mythic structure of the Hero's Journey sends a Hero away from home and onto a path into an unknown world, punctuated by moments of terror and wonder, culminating in a climactic experience that irrevocably changes the Hero, who returns home wiser, stronger, and capable of helping the next Hero with his or her own journey of self-discovery. We can see the Hero's Journey reflected in our lives anytime we seek out or go along with a new experience. And as writers, we see it every time we embark on the writing process with a new project.

> *A Hero is a person who says yes to the adventure.*

Are you a person who says yes to the adventure? If you've picked up this book, you've already done that.

A Hero is a person who is connected with his or her own inherent gifts.

Time to start writing. Open your blank book or journal to the first page.

On one side of the page, write down the names of three people—living or dead, real or fictitious, it's up to you—whom you most aspire to be like.

On the other side of the page, write down the three qualities you most admire in each person.

Now, fold the page in half so only the character traits, not the names, are showing.

How many of these qualities do you already possess?

A mentor of mine used this exercise years ago to show me how much easier it is to recognize the attributes we admire in others than in ourselves. But so often, the people we most long to be like, our heroes, are simply versions of ourselves that are further along in life than we are, or who've employed the qualities we share with them to take a different path than we have so far. To forge our own paths, we have to understand what our natural gifts and strengths are and foster them with our attention.

Just like the people you admire, you have inherent qualities that might already be inspiring others. It's your choice what to do with them.

You are a Hero.

Heroes exhibit three kinds of behavior that I suspect you already do.

1. PROTECT

The Greek root of the word "hero" means "to protect and serve." In myth, Heroes often embark on journeys in a quest to protect something precious to them—a person, a place, a way of life.

Throughout this book, we'll be exploring ways for you to protect something very precious to you: your writing. We're going to nourish your work itself, from its most nascent stages to a polished project you release into the world. Protecting your writing means creating a personalized way of working that is sturdy but flexible, so developing your process will be at the heart of the work we'll do.

Heroes model for us what it means to be in process. When we meet our favorite Heroes, they are just at the beginning of an ordeal, like writers starting a project. They show us how to get through a series of challenges and come out the other side wiser and stronger.

We'll look at how to protect your writing time as sacred, how to bolster yourself with support from other people, and how to guard your psyche from the pitfalls you're most susceptible to.

As you embark on this journey, think about what else in your life needs protection. What parts of yourself are vulnerable, tender, or at risk? Is there an area where you feel helpless or frustrated and wish a Hero would swoop in and rescue you?

By the end of this journey, you'll be equipped to be your own Hero, a strong protector.

2. SERVE

Service is also at the heart of every Hero's Journey. Rather than acting solely out of ego, Heroes serve a cause greater than the self. The cause could be as grandiose as saving the world or as contained as helping one person, but for the Hero, the purpose is for some greater good.

Writing can feel like a self-focused act. To do it, we have to take ourselves away from other people. We're working on projects that express our personal visions, which we dare to believe others will find interesting. We make time for writing at the expense of acts that seem to serve others—spending time with loved ones, caring for our children, volunteering, participating in our communities, keeping our homes from looking like Superfund site candidates. We isolate ourselves from communication, ignoring phone, email, and social media (or at least, we try to), and can even begin to lose our deeper connections to other people. Talking about feeling alienated from his peers, author Rick Moody told me, "My classmates from high school and college were all moving into genteel middle age, and I was still making ramen noodles and holing up for weeks at a time. It was great for writing novels, but probably stunted my emotional maturation."

Being a Hero in your writing journey means balancing the self-focus that is essential for writing with a sense of a broader purpose. You're not writing in a vacuum, to amuse yourself, or simply because you want people to pay attention to you. You're writing because you have something to say that you feel *needs* to be said.

What is it about this story or message that burns to be told—and by you, specifically? What do you want to add to the world with this piece of writing? Ezra Pound called artists "the antennae of the race"; what are you picking up on your antenna and translating into a message that people need to hear? Whom are you hoping to reach, perhaps to show them they're not the only ones who feel the way they do, that they're not alone in the world?

What greater cause are you serving by being a writer? If you don't have a ready answer right now, you may by the end of this chapter.

3. SACRIFICE

To achieve their goals, Heroes in myth must make sacrifices. They give up the comfort of home to go on an adventure, and they often have to let go of even more—sometimes the person or thing they love most—in order to reach what they seek.

I'm sure you've already experienced the sacrifice that being a writer involves. You become a time thief, pilfering minutes or hours from everything else you need or want to do and sacrificing it to your writing. You loosen your connection to society, withdrawing to be alone with your work, sometimes even losing the people in your life who don't understand your need to pursue this isolating passion. Sometimes, you sacrifice your sanity or the appearance of sanity; you catch yourself talking out loud to one of your characters while at the grocery store, or have to excuse yourself in the middle of a party to furiously scribble notes before you forget the idea you just had.

And if you came to this book because you've been struggling to fit writing into your life, you may need to sacrifice even more. Over the coming chapters, we'll be looking at what elements of your life you can nudge out of the way to clear more space for your writing, and how to make it a higher priority.

But in exchange for the sacrifices you make, you get a priceless gift.

A comedian told me about a fellow up-and-coming comic who was performing at Manhattan's famed Comedy Cellar when Chris Rock happened to show up. After the show, she got the opportunity to share a few drinks with the comedy legend. One of his statements particularly stuck with her. Chris Rock said, "I never found myself in a hole I couldn't write myself out of."

As challenging and frustrating as writing can be, it is also a lifeline. It's something you can do anywhere, under any circumstances, and bend to any purpose. A musician needs her instrument, an actor needs his script, an artist needs materials like paints, brushes, or—depending on the artist—elephant poop, but a writer can create using the most basic tools. We may believe we need our computers, but entire novels have been written on cell phones, and in a pinch, a pen and paper still work just fine. From those simple tools, whole worlds are born.

> *Chris Rock said, "I never found myself in a hole I couldn't write myself out of."*

To write is to be a wizard, creating something out of nothing. Being a writer, and a Hero, means being a creator. And if you didn't believe it was worth the sacrifices, you wouldn't be here.

Let's look at how to begin the work of protecting, serving, and sacrificing that will help you start your own Hero's Journey.

Who Are You?

Every good story begins with a great character. Whether we're reading a book, watching a film or show, fiction or nonfiction, we need to care about the main character from the very beginning or we won't enjoy the ride. When you're writing a character, you need to know as much as possible about your subject—even things that don't make the final cut—in order to write authentically and vividly about this person.

In the Hero's Journey of your own process, you need to know everything you can about the Hero—you—before you embark. The exercise that follows is designed to help you identify your strengths, recognize your vulnerabilities, and clarify your mission as a writer. It will also help you figure out which chapters of this book may be most helpful to you right now.

And we'll do all that with the help of a game best known for being played by Vitamin D-deficient teenagers in basements.

Inspired by role-playing games like Dungeons & Dragons, this exercise will reveal what kind of Hero you are.

EXERCISE: CHARACTER SHEET

Create a visual representation of your avatar. It can be as realistic or as imaginative as you like. You could pick a fictional character you admire or simply find an image that resonates. Whatever you choose, it should reflect who you want to be and how you intend to see yourself on this creative journey.

NAME: Choose a Hero name.

MISSION STATEMENT: Why do you write? What do you want your writing to accomplish? Write a one-sentence mission statement that ties your work, or the motivation behind it, together.

PROJECT VISION: What is your vision for this specific project? Why is it important to you? What do you hope it will contribute to the world? Why does this story need telling? Write a one-sentence vision statement for the project.

HISTORY: Give a brief bio of yourself.

SKILLS: Rate yourself on a scale of 1–5 (1 being worst, 5 being best) in the following categories with regard to your writing process. Be honest, not brutal.

- Inspiration: Getting a lot of ideas that excite you and spark your imagination.

- Connection: Asking for help or support when you need it.

- Intuition: Listening to and following your gut when making decisions.

- Focus: Resisting distractions, insecurities, and other challenges to focus.

- Resilience: Pushing through the stage(s) of the writing process that most challenge you (i.e., getting started, getting through the first section, crossing the desert of the middle, finishing what you start, revising).

- Patience: Dealing with going through a fallow period.

- Courage: Overcoming adversity and setbacks and turning them into opportunities for growth.

- Flexibility: Shifting between different modes of thinking or action, i.e., between drafting and revising.

- Confidence: Feeling secure about your work, your ability to execute your vision, and yourself.

- Based on the scores you gave yourself on SKILLS, note your GREATEST STRENGTH and your GREATEST VULNERABILITY and highlight them.

GEAR: What are the tools you use for your writing process? Think beyond your computer: Do you have a favorite location to do work? An old hoodie you like to wear while writing? Books you like to have nearby that inspire you?

ENERGY FUEL: What fuels and energizes you when you're writing? (I.e., coffee, tea, snacks, music, writing with a certain friend)

ENERGY DRAINS: What sucks away your energy when you're writing? (I.e., being distracted by your phone, falling into an Internet hole, social media)

TREASURE: What is your treasure? What is the special gift you carry with you wherever you go, that writing helps you share with the world?

When you've completed your Character Sheet, you may want to post it somewhere prominent, where you'll see it when you sit down to write.

We'll come back to these character traits throughout the book, and use this exercise as a blueprint for the work you'll be doing on your process.

Your First Step

Now that you're aware of your strengths, what do you want to apply them to first? I don't want you to have to wait until you're deeper into the book to begin the work you came here to do; let's start it today.

What challenge, struggle, or obstacle in your writing brought you to this book? What aspect of your process do you most want to develop? What is the Achilles' heel you want to address—not next week, not once you've finished reading the whole book, but *right now*?

If the answer you filled in for GREATEST VULNERABILITY resonated with you, that's probably the place to begin.

So how do you start to tackle an issue that may have been dogging you for years? If this were a coaching session, the work would unfold in our discussion. Speaking about a problem has been proven to help us all—that's why talk therapy remains the most popular form of therapy. According to storytelling scholar Jonathan Gottschall, studies have shown that talk therapy can sometimes work as well as, and in certain cases better than, more recent developments like antidepressant drugs or cognitive behavioral therapy.

But numerous psychology studies have also shown that writing about an issue or traumatic event improved participants' psychological states and even physical health. If you already keep a journal yourself, you've probably experienced those benefits.

As a writer, you're fortunate that writing-as-therapy comes built into the process of creating your art. But there are ways to use it that go beyond journaling. Let's apply it strategically to the most pressing challenge you're facing in your process.

EXERCISE: EXPLORING YOUR VULNERABILITY

This exercise is adapted from the work of psychologist James W. Pennebaker, who has been studying writing-as-therapy for over a decade. Even if you already keep a journal, you should set aside time specifically for this exercise in addition to your usual journal-writing time.

Begin with the trait you listed as your greatest vulnerability in the Character Sheet exercise. If you rated yourself a "1" in more than one category, pick the one that's causing you the most anxiety or affecting your writing most on a day-to-day basis.

For the next five days, beginning today, set aside at least fifteen minutes that are yours and yours alone, uninterrupted and undisturbed, when you can be by yourself.

During each of these fifteen-minute periods, write about the trait you selected. You can take that direction and run with it, or you can use one or more of the following prompts to get you started:

- What does it feel like to struggle with this vulnerability?

- How has this issue manifested itself in the past?

- Is there a connection between this issue and your childhood, past relationship(s), or your career?

- Did any particular event bring on your difficulty in this area?

- If you had to tell the deep, dark truth about this part of yourself, what would that be?

You'll notice that none of these prompts steers you toward finding a solution. For these five consecutive days, allow yourself not to focus on your desire to resolve the issue and just experience the feeling of being inside the issue itself.

At the end of the five days, read over what you have written. The words you've put down are for your eyes only, but you may want to use what you've gleaned from doing the exercise to start a discussion with your writing peers. Or you may prefer to keep your thoughts on this to yourself. Do whatever feels safest for you, recognizing that the work you have undertaken is important, challenging, and ongoing.

The Secret to Turning Goals into Action

There is no single, silver-bullet way to accomplish a goal in the timeline you want to do it in. But we can learn from other people who've met their goals.

British psychologist Richard Wiseman ran two studies that tracked five thousand participants all over the world who were working toward achieving a range of goals. He followed half for six months and half for a year, and paid close attention as they endeavored to quit smoking, lose weight, recycle more, and so on—the same kinds of goals that many of us pursue rigorously for about two weeks every January and then promptly give up on.

At the end of the studies, he found that only about ten percent of the participants reported they'd succeeded in accomplishing what they set out to do.

So what were the methods that worked for these five hundred people? They shared the goal with others (which we'll talk about in chapter three). They rewarded themselves for progress and thought about the positive effects of achieving the goal, both of which we'll also discuss later in the book.

And they made a step-by-step plan and recorded their progress. Instead of setting an ambitious but vague goal and leaving it at that, they outlined all the incremental actions they'd need to take in order to get that new job or change those habits.

I've seen this step-by-step planning work for writers like Marta.

Marta was leading a double life. By day, she worked as a doctor. But she had a dirty secret: early in the morning, before heading to her office, she spent two hours several days a week in a greasy-spoon diner, nursing a cup of coffee and working on her novel.

When I began coaching Marta, she knew she wanted to finish her manuscript, but didn't have a clear vision for how that was going to happen. She'd been chipping away at it for over a year and had gotten about halfway through, but she worried she'd be working on it forever.

It was May, so we began by setting a due date of October first. This was the day when she would send the manuscript out to editors. We tied her personal due date to an outward-facing action, to give it additional accountability.

Then, we worked backward from that date, establishing everything she would need to accomplish in order to have a polished manuscript that she felt good about by October first. She wanted to share the manuscript with her critique group, get their feedback, and then revise it before sending it out, so we built in time for her group to read it and the following revision. Before that, she would be drafting, which involved both writing and research, so we planned time for both.

Laying out her plans in this way, we carved a path that took us right from the day we were having our discussion. The next morning, when she rolled up to the diner at six a.m., she'd know exactly what she needed to do in order to stay on schedule.

Any voyage is difficult without a map. Whether you let GPS do the navigating for you or prefer to rely on atlases and good old-fashioned road maps that are impossible to perfectly fold up ever again, having a sense of how you're getting where you're going is essential.

Mapping out your goals, and how you plan to achieve them, doesn't mean you're then stuck with what you've outlined. Even if you were just using a map on a road trip, you'd still be able to take a detour to see the World's Largest Ball of Fishing Twine if you got a yen for it along the way. But a map gives you a framework to contain both your planned actions and your detours, putting each leg of the journey into context, reminding you where you've been and how far you have yet to go, and keeping you from straying too far from any path that leads to your primary objective.

Here's an example of the map for Marta's project.

First, she set her primary goal at the center: sending the manuscript to editors.

Knowing she had a deadline and a destination in mind, she worked backward to figure out when she'd need to give the manuscript to her critique group so they'd have enough time to read it and give her feedback and she would have time to revise before she sent it out:

Before sharing it with anyone, though, Marta wanted to have a chance to revise the whole manuscript from the first draft, so she built that in as well.

Then, working backward from the date she wanted to start revising, she broke her process out into multiple paths. The book required research, which she wanted to do simultaneously with writing new chapters, so she made these paths run parallel to one another, terminating at the same end date.

She backed up until she got to the day she was making the map.

Then, I had her back up even further, to include all the work she had already done to get to that point. Unless you are creating this map on the very day you first conceive the idea for the project, it's likely that you've already done some work. In Marta's case, she had written about half of her manuscript and done some research. Adding those accomplishments expanded her map and placed her much further along in the journey than the proverbial square one, where she'd felt like she was.

She tried to make the map as specific as possible, to include minutiae like what hours she'd write on which days, to make it a kind of schedule for herself. The more accurate she was, the easier she found it to follow.

When Marta first completed her map, I thought she'd be relieved and calmed, but much to my surprise, her first response was panic.

"I have so much to do before the deadline!" she exclaimed. "How can I ever get it done in time?"

But when I checked in with her two weeks later, she was in a completely different frame of mind. Once she began completing tasks and moving closer to her goal, she discovered how much more satisfying it was to track her progress, rather than just inching forward with no sense of how far she had left to go.

Studies have shown that people who know what to expect are often happier and calmer than those facing the formless unknown. With this map to guide you, you're more likely to feel some measure of control over your process.

EXERCISE: MAPPING YOUR JOURNEY

Following Marta's example, choose a concrete, time-bound project goal, such as, *Finish the first draft of my novel by September 15.* You can apply the map to any tangible goal, but I'll be referring to it mainly as a way to plot a route to a completed draft.

Then, as Marta did, work backward and use milestones to create a timeline that is realistic for you and takes into account your schedule and the time you can spend writing. Make sure to include multiple paths if you are doing more than the actual drafting—you can include research, interviews, reading, and anything else that contributes to your project.

After you've set all your goals, it's time to choose a reward. Think about something special you would like to do for yourself when you have completed the whole map and reached the project goal. Make it something that is truly a treat, that you don't normally get to do or have. Write it down beside your goal.

You can make your map small and keep it in a notebook; make it big and hang it in your workspace; create it digitally and keep the file open when you're writing.

You may interact with your map in whatever way you choose. You might prefer to simply have it around, but if you'd like to have a more active relationship with it, you might block out your route along each path in measurable squares and color in each one as you accomplish the task it contains.

You should also consider this map a living document; it can absolutely be changed along the way. Dates can be adjusted; paths can be added or removed; even the primary goal might change. This journey will take you places you weren't expecting to go. But plotting a route at the beginning will make those detours and surprises more manageable.

As you can see, the map also resembles a game board. Another way to interact with your map is to make a playing piece (or multiple pieces, if you have multiple paths) that you can stick onto the map and advance just like when playing a game. If you do this, you can use your Character Sheet for inspiration to create a playing piece that embodies who you are on this journey.

I'm sure you will come up with your own creative ways to build, use, and enjoy this map of your Hero's Journey. And we'll revisit it when we get farther down the road.

Your Life Is a Journey

When I call you a Hero, I'm not just talking about your writing process. You're a Hero in the story of your life. When we see our lives as stories, we give ourselves a way to understand and deal with the moments of joy and adversity that we inevitably go through.

The last place Javier had expected to be at age twenty-three was jail. He'd been a good student and had plans to get his GED and pursue a career in technology. A young father supporting his child, wife, and mother, Javier had been making money the way many people in his Bronx neighborhood did: on the corner. Not everybody got caught, but he had, and was facing jail time. Sitting under house arrest, waiting for a judge to hear his case, he could already see life's doors closing on him.

Hoping to improve his situation, Javier enrolled in a class run by a program that helps those who've been arrested but not yet convicted for federal crimes. For twelve weeks, the group met each Tuesday evening in a conference room at a New York City courthouse. With a range of ages, backgrounds, and arrest records, the students shared one common bond: they were all waiting for the trials that would determine their fates.

One day in class, another student was talking about his fears: that he would be locked up, miss years of his children's lives while in prison, damage his relationship with his wife.

Javier was the youngest student in the group, but he spoke up to comfort his classmate. He admitted he was scared, and that he had no idea what the future would bring. But, he said, this period in his life—in all their lives—was temporary. He could already see the other side of his waiting time, and even his jail time, as a chapter of his life still waiting to be written. He talked about life being long and using this as a chance to turn his in a different direction.

By seeing himself as a Hero on a journey, Javier could transform the experience of his arrest into the turning point that set him on a path toward becoming a more fully realized person.

I've taught women and men in prison and on house arrest since 2012. Time and time again, I've witnessed that those who were able to see their lives as a journey were better able to handle whatever came their way, and could salvage some value from life's dark moments.

In an examination of scientific evidence of what makes people happy, psychologist Timothy D. Wilson identified three key elements to a happy life as *meaning*, *hope*, and *purpose*. The happiest and most fulfilled people, he said, can find a way to extract meaning or make sense of bad things that happen, believe that good things will happen, and see themselves as Heroes on a journey to accomplish goals they have set. Those who view themselves as the protagonists in their own stories, "who feel in control of their lives, have goals of their own choosing, and make progress toward those goals—are happier than people who do not."

We are all subject to circumstance, and some measure of misfortune gets sprinkled or dumped into each life. But we have a choice about how to react to that misfortune and how to answer those questions I raised earlier in the chapter—*Who am I? What am I on this earth to do?*

When I taught a class on the Hero's Journey at a women's prison, we had a discussion about how Heroes in stories often make mistakes. One of my students pointed to the board where we'd just listed "heroic qualities"—*loyal, brave, willing to sacrifice, cares about bigger cause, hardworking.*

"So a Hero could be all those things," she asked, "and still fuck up?"

A Hero is not someone who has always made wise choices, who unfailingly does the right thing, who is endlessly selfless and giving— far from it. No matter how deep our flaws, how regretful we feel about past actions, we can always see ourselves as Heroes moving through a dark chapter toward brighter days and hope.

You decide who you are. You decide what you are on this earth to do.

Just like the woman who asked that question, you have a choice in how to see yourself: Criminal or student. Irredeemable or flawed-but-learning. Someone who made bad choices or someone whose choices yielded wisdom.

You decide who you are. You decide what you are on this earth to do. And you define what part of your life's journey you are in right now and what kind of Hero you are in the face of it.

Looking at the narrative of your life in a new way is part of what therapy and coaching are all about. Says Jonathan Gottschall, "A psychotherapist can . . . be seen as a kind of script doctor who helps patients revise their life stories so that they can play the role of protagonists again—suffering and flawed protagonists, to be sure, but protagonists who are moving toward the light." If you are seeking a different way to perceive the story of your own life, the archetypes we'll explore in the coming chapters will open doors to new ways of seeing—and experiencing—that story.

You Are a Hero

If you're feeling like a Hero, read on. If you aren't, read on, because there's so much more ahead to help you become the writer you were born to be. Over the chapters that follow, we're going to take everything you did in chapter one and use it to put your identified gifts to good use, strengthen your vulnerable areas, accomplish the goal or goals you laid out, and embody your mission as a writer. Let's take every storytelling tool we can find together and apply them not only to your work, but to your life, and to the place where those two are intertwined. Let's make this chapter of your life one of exploration, self-discovery, and clarity in the face of challenge.

Let's say yes to the adventure and embark on it together.

CHAPTER TWO

the herald

follow and create
inspiration and change

Where do you get your ideas?

If you've ever attended a reading or panel of writers, watched or listened to an author being interviewed, or scrolled through an online Q&A of a famous writer, chances are you've seen this question posed. And if you happen to be a writer who has given a reading, spoken on a panel, or been interviewed in any forum, you've absolutely been asked this question. It's the most common query, and one that can fill authors with dread.

Because the most truthful answer is usually *I don't know.*

Where do ideas come from? What makes us sit bolt upright in the middle of the night and madly scribble on the nearest available surface, or interrupts us in the middle of an important meeting or a family gathering with a phrase, a conceit, a plotline we must put to paper immediately before it floats away?

Call it the muse, inspiration, or whatever you like, but it's the part of us that sees or hears some snippet of life and thinks, *That would make a good story.*

In this book, we'll call it the **Herald**. While it may seem elusive and unwieldy to control, we'll examine a handful of ways to tame it to bring you ideas for new projects that excite and feel true to you and turn them into the concrete beginning of a project. And this archetype can ultimately inspire change in your life beyond your writing process.

The Call to Adventure

In myth, the Herald is a messenger who brings the Hero the "call to adventure," an invitation to leave the familiar world of home behind and embark on a dangerous but exciting quest. Heralds are agents of change; they signal to Heroes that life, which may have been dull but familiar up to this point, is about to carry them in a totally new direction.

For writers, the Herald is the patron saint of beginnings. When the first seed of an idea lands in your mind and starts to take root, that's the Herald's voice you're hearing, calling you to the adventure of a new writing project.

The Herald is what distinguishes writers from the rest of the population. Other people see a funny photo a friend posted online; you see a story idea. They see an item on the news; you see a subject you're itching to research and write about. They see an interaction between strangers; you see two characters whose backstories are begging to be explored. Wherever you go, the Herald in you is seeking the narrative, the juice, the inspiration in the everyday. It's the part of you that's always listening for a story.

Wherever you go, the Herald in you is seeking the narrative, the juice, the inspiration in the everyday.

We're going to look at five different ways to invite the Herald into your life. By the end of this chapter, you won't need to ask the writers you admire "How do you get your ideas?"—you'll have a whole stable of methods for getting them yourself. And if you didn't already come to this book with a project underway, you'll have heeded the Herald's call to get started on your next piece of writing.

But first, let's do a quick exercise to see what the Herald has brought you in the past to get some clues about where your Herald could take you next.

the hero is you

EXERCISE: HEARING THE HERALD'S CALL

In this exercise, we're going to take a look at your ideas—old and new—and see what's inspiring you.

In the context of this exercise, the term "idea" refers to a concept, however loose, that forms the premise of a project. Some examples of what we're calling "ideas": "story about a man who travels from China to Sweden in search of his runaway daughter, who turns out to have transitioned to male"; "nonfiction piece about women in professional wrestling"; "sci fi set in a world where time travel is commonplace." (You'll notice that ideas can be plot-driven, character-driven, or setting-driven—and you might have ideas of all three kinds.)

- Write down at least three ideas you had more than a year ago that you haven't written yet—the older, the better, and include as many as you can think of.

- Write down up to three ideas you've had within the last year that you haven't explored yet.

- If you are currently focused on a project already, describe it in a single sentence like the examples given above.

Beside each of the ideas you wrote, describe how you got the idea (i.e., from something you read, heard, saw, it came to you in a dream, based on a real-life experience you had, or other ways).

- Write down the titles of one to three books, movies, TV shows, plays, or other media that made you think, *I wish I'd had that idea!*

Do you notice any theme(s) linking all the ideas you included? If so, what? Do you notice any pattern(s) to how you find your ideas? If so, what?

Here's what we'll do with this information.

- YOUR OLD IDEAS: There's a reason you kept these in a file somewhere, and if you were able to remember them off the top of your head, that's all the more evidence: these ideas have resonance for you. Just because you haven't used them yet doesn't mean you won't. You might explore one exactly as-is, or you could find that, as you make your way through this book, you want to combine ideas, blend one into a different project, or draw from them in other ways. They're a valuable resource to keep on hand.

- YOUR RECENT IDEAS: If you didn't come to this book with a project already underway, pay especially close attention to these, because one of them may become the one you focus on. If you're already in the middle of something else, you never know how these ideas might inform your current work or spark the project that follows it—or the one you develop on the side when you need to take breaks from your primary project.

- HOW YOU GOT YOUR IDEAS: The better understanding you have of what's inspired you in the past, the more you can use that information to find inspiration in the future.

- WRITING YOU ADMIRE: Looking at the work of the writers we most admire can be intimidating when we're feeling vulnerable, but it can also give us clues about what kinds of ideas most excite us, and what kinds of challenges we'd be most charged up by taking on. If you notice that your answers for this question revealed more ambition than your past ideas—for example, if all your past ideas are for realistic, pulled-from-life stories, but the ideas you wished you'd had were high-concept or highly imaginative (say, a movie like *Avatar* or book like *The Parable of the Sower*)—then maybe it's time to challenge yourself by writing something more fanciful than what's constituted your comfort zone thus far.

Inviting the Herald

Mythological Heroes are often surprised by the appearance of a Herald, but that doesn't mean you have to wait around for inspiration to strike you with an idea when you least expect it. There are many ways to create ideal conditions for ideas to emerge, and to seek them out.

1. BE OPEN

A truism among New Yorkers is that you can tell the tourists from the locals because the tourists are always looking up. But even a New Yorker determined to blend in will be the one with the craned neck when visiting Tokyo, Istanbul, or Johannesburg. Being a foreigner in a new place turns our observational powers on and makes us notice what, at home, we'd brush right by. It puts us in a state more like children, who look around with curiosity, seeking out the interesting, the new, and often the potentially edible.

As a writer, it's your responsibility to be a traveler in your own hometown, a child in your adult life. Walking through the world as if you were on vacation or exploring it for the first time will reveal to you the potential stories hidden within what may look completely mundane. Some of the most compelling human drama I've witnessed has occurred between strangers at the restaurant table next to mine or the adjacent pump at a gas station.

As a writer, it's your responsibility to be a traveler in your own hometown, a child in your adult life.

Since the advent of smartphones, most Americans now walk around carrying tiny cameras at all times. But writers have always had tiny cameras to record the strange, poignant, or hilarious moments that life spontaneously yields up. The Herald is that camera, recording kernels of conflict (the couple having a fight on a corner), humor (the pint-sized lady with the enormous dog, both wrapped in matching pink chinchilla jackets), and curiosity (a poster that simply says "SAY YES") that could germinate and blossom into a story.

College student Bijou Goldfarb normally followed the unspoken city-dweller code when it came to pamphleteers and canvassers: eyes down, a polite but firm "no thanks," and keep moving briskly along. But the shaggy-haired, undeniably handsome young man in the JESUS SAVES T-shirt was so striking, she broke her rule and accepted the tract he thrust at her, even though she was Jewish and had no interest in being saved, by Jesus or anyone else.

She stuffed the pamphlet in her bag and forgot about it until later that day, when she was stuck on a bus in rush-hour gridlock. Seeking a distraction from the suffocating closeness of the armpit forest, she dug the fundamentalist leaflet out of her handbag and began to read.

Bijou didn't get born again, but she did get an idea. *What if God were a gay teenager?* she mused. Squashed against the bus wall, she began to write the first lines of the wildly irreverent take on the creation myth that would become her thesis project.

Being open—even to something she thought she had no interest in—created a space for a fresh idea to blossom.

So keep your eyes open to the world around you. No matter how boring or familiar you believe your environment is, if you examine it with the eyes of a tourist or a child, you can find enough material on any given day to spin into a story that activates your imagination.

MINI-EXERCISE CHALLENGE

The next time a stranger starts talking to you, don't brush past or hang up the phone—take five minutes to engage in conversation and see what this person has to say. Or initiate your own chat with a stranger who crosses your path. (Obviously, do this only in situations you feel are safe.) Then document the conversation in your journal.

---

2. BE A CULTURAL CONSUMER

One of your responsibilities as an artist is to pay attention to the work of other artists. Google "advice for writers" and you're sure to find that most well-known writers encourage aspirants in the field to read, read, read. Read in the area you're writing and outside of it; read stuff you love and stuff you don't; read the classics and the latest emerging work. Read it all.

It's just as important to be attuned to the creations of other kinds of artists. Listening to music, looking at visual art in its many forms, watching a dance performance, playing a video game—the possibilities are endless, and full of endless potential to inspire you.

In her famed book on creativity, *The Artist's Way*, author Julia Cameron encourages writers to go on "artist's dates," seeking out new experiences and cultural fulfillment in order to "fill the well" of inspiration with potential fodder. She first published that book in 1992, before the Internet had fully opened up its rabbit hole of information and we tumbled into an impossibly vast and abundant Wonderland of entertainment, interaction, education, and convenience (and, course, distraction). You can access the contents of the Louvre, go on a virtual tour of Yellowstone, enroll in a course on any subject from astral projection to zoology, all without putting on pants.

The Internet is a wonderful resource for the Herald. Writers used to pore over the newspapers they subscribed to for ideas; now we can scroll through any news source in the world for free before getting out of bed. Plug any random word into YouTube and you can dip into a vast sea of human nature on display. Even social media can provide inspiration; children's author Janet Fox got the idea that inspired her critically acclaimed middle grade novel *The Charmed Children of Rookskill Castle* from a photo of an antique piece of jewelry her friend posted on Facebook.

At the same time, the Internet is no replacement for the world IRL. Online activity doesn't feed all five senses, and even the most emotionally intense web interaction takes place with a buffer between you and the experience. Anything online can instantly disappear with a single click the moment you want it to go away. The unpredictable, inescapable nature of in-the-world experiences gives them a greater immediacy and resonance, which can make them a stronger foundation for your writing.

It's not wrong to fuel your Herald with online explorations, but it's ideal to balance them by leaving your home to find and consume art, too.

The Cooper Hewitt Smithsonian Design Museum in New York City lends its visitors a small wand on entry. Called a "Pen" and resembling one, this device is catnip for people who hate to forget what they see. You can carry it around the museum and when you see something you want to remember or explore further, you zap its coded label with the Pen, which will store information about each item you scan to create your own personalized "collection" of what you've seen, to later view online.

Writers must have their own mental version of this magic wand. However you like to retain the art you absorb—by taking notes, snapping a photo, journaling about it, researching it online and filing that information away—it's important to save reminders of the culture you've consumed and anything you see that sparks you. You never know when a seed of inspiration might bear fruit.

In 1940, then-struggling children's illustrator Ezra Jack Keats cut a series of photos out of *Life* magazine of a little boy being administered a vaccination and pinned it to his wall because he liked the boy's facial expressions and thought he might be a good model for a future illustration. But time passed and no art directors asked Keats for an illustration that included an African American child. The clipping sat on Keats' wall for twenty years before Keats decided if he wanted to see the little boy appear in a story, he'd have to write it himself. The book he wrote and illustrated was *The Snowy Day*, which would go on to become one of the best-loved classics of children's literature.

Consume as much culture as you can—of all kinds—and find a way to collect it so you'll have a dragon's hoard of nuggets to foster future inspiration.

Consume as much culture as you can—of all kinds—and find a way to collect it so you'll have a dragon's hoard of nuggets to foster future inspiration.

3. PUT YOURSELF OUT THERE

You don't have to venture far afield to find inspiration for your writing. Author Robert Cormier lived his entire life in Leominster, Massachusetts, and published seventeen novels. Emily Dickinson is one of the most famous poets in Western literature and barely even left her bedroom.

Traveling, though, is a wonderful way to leave our comfort zones and discover the world, and unexplored aspects of ourselves, by being in a new environment. Going anywhere you haven't been before, even if it's just a part of your town that's not on your usual route, will show you fresh sights that can be fodder for the Herald.

So can pursuing any new experience. One writer I know took up archery after a knee injury aborted her daily running practice, and learning about this sport she'd hardly known existed wound up inspiring a novel. You don't have to wait for an injury or trauma to force you into learning a new skill or trying a new activity.

And of course, some of the greatest ideas come to us through the people we meet. Extend yourself beyond your usual social circles and connect with people who have different interests, backgrounds, life experiences, and worldviews from your own. You don't have to love every one of them, but see each one—even those you disagree with—as possessing value for you through the experience of meeting.

The places we see, the experiences we have, the people we meet—they all fuel the Herald.

Set aside four hours to visit a place you've never been or take a class in a skill you've never attempted. Bonus points if you strike up a conversation with a stranger while doing either! Write a description of the experience in your journal.

---

4. MINE YOUR OWN HISTORY

In *Bird by Bird,* author and teacher Anne Lamott suggests readers seeking inspiration begin by describing the lunches of their school years. Poet Rainer Maria Rilke called childhood "that jewel beyond price, that treasurehouse of memories," saying that even if we were trapped in a cell with no access to the outside world, we'd still have an endless source of inspiration in our past. (How motivated you'd be to work on your memoirs if you found yourself in this situation is questionable, though Nelson Mandela managed it under just about the worst conditions imaginable.)

We are able to wrap our heads around our lives by turning their events into stories we tell ourselves. Those stories can seep into our writing as straight memoir, as fictionalized versions of themselves, blended and composited, dissected for details, or even simply the emotional truth of the experiences of our past applied to entirely different situations (to me, the actual meaning of the old saw, "write what you know"). One of the great gifts of being a writer is that every experience can become material.

After dropping out of college, walking the Pacific Crest Trail from Mexico to Canada, and along the way, meeting the man who became her husband, Aspen Matis had moved to New York, looking to break into journalism. Her husband was supporting her while she studied at the New School under bestselling author Susan Shapiro.

Aspen had written about her epic walk for the first assignment in her class with Susan, but had left out what had motivated her to take the trek. When Susan pressed her, saying the heart of the story seemed to be missing, Aspen revealed the real reason she'd walked the PCT: her second night of college, a boy in her dorm had raped her, and she'd fled to the trail as a way to heal her wounded psyche.

Aspen was afraid to write about her experience, but Susan encouraged her to use the essay to work through her trauma instead of hiding that part of the story. Writing what had happened to her turned out to be cathartic for Aspen, and it brought the big break she'd been seeking. Aspen's essay "A Hiker's Guide to Healing" was published in the Modern Love column in the *New York Times* and turned into a memoir, *Girl in the Woods*, which was published in 2015. The television rights were optioned and the TV series went into development before the book was even out.

Whether you're writing to process some wound from your past or simply extracting elements of your life to season your work, there is great richness in the years behind you.

MINI-EXERCISE CHALLENGE

Pick an episode from your childhood that you've never written about before and spend ten minutes describing it in detail. It doesn't have to be a major or traumatic moment; it could be a very simple memory. Don't worry about accuracy—focus more on the emotional truth than the literal details. It's okay to flesh it out with some fictional set-dressing.

5. RESTRICTIONS ARE YOUR FRIEND

Writing for daily television is a crucible that forces writers to throw the idea of waiting for the muse out the window. If you find yourself postponing writing because you're waiting for inspiration to strike, imagine if your livelihood depended on you writing—and writing *now*.

Negin Farsad was stumped. She had been sitting in the writers' room at MTV all day with her colleagues, trying to come up with a good joke about a competitive dance reality show. But for whatever reason, the comedy well had run dry, and the only jokes she could think of were so weak, they didn't even bear repeating.

Negin and her colleagues were writers on a daily entertainment news show. They began each workday by sitting down with the day's newspaper and all the latest entertainment news arrayed in front of them and picking items that sparked ideas for jokes, which they'd bandy about the table. The show runner would pay close attention to which jokes seemed to pop and direct various writers to follow those threads. They spent the morning writing, and the show would tape in the afternoon and air that evening.

That particular day, the crew had gone ahead and recorded the show. But at five p.m., when the writers had already downed gallons of coffee and were well beyond burnout, the director came back into the writers' room. She told the team, in no uncertain terms, that nobody was leaving the room until they'd come up with a better joke about the dance show to give to the host, tape, and include in the evening's show.

All Negin wanted was to go home, order some chicken pad thai, and watch a few episodes of *Arrested Development*. But she knew if she didn't get inspired—stat—she could lose her job.

To call the Herald to visit her, Negin dug into her "bag of tricks." As a comedy writer, she knew there were certain formats for telling jokes that she and her colleagues used frequently. Many comedy writers have told me that when they can't spontaneously come up with something funny about, say, the presidential election, they can always reverse-engineer a joke: pick a format and inject the presidential election into it.

In Negin's bag of tricks were formats like creating a genre parody ("So You Think You Can Joust"—a competitive reality show set in Westeros), finding a connection between the subject and another current event (Vladimir Putin Guest Stars on *America's Got Talent*, but is eliminated when he is caught trying to have all the other contestants sent to a Siberian gulag), or doing additional research on the subject at hand (Did you know that the classic ballroom dancing stance was originally a result of the man wearing a sword on one side of his belt?). If you think

the hero is you

these examples don't deserve to make it onto TV, that's why I don't write for television.

Negin tried a few of these joke formats before wondering how she could satirize the show using a funny juxtaposition or analogy. *What is a competitive ballroom dancing reality show analogous to?* she asked herself. Then, it hit her: a boxing championship.

She created a silly send-up of the show, listing the dancers' weight classes, having the commentators talk about their sparring records, and now that she had the general idea, all the pieces began to fall into place.

The joke ran, the show taped, and everyone got to go home that night with jobs intact. And then they got up the next morning and did it again.

Thinking *I need a great idea* over and over doesn't tend to be very helpful when you're struggling to have a brain wave; just seeking a "great idea" is too broad, too unwieldy, too vague. But if you give yourself a format or restrictions to pour your great idea into, the possibilities get narrowed down and suddenly it's a lot easier to get inspired.

EXERCISE: TV PACKETS

When comedy writers are trying to get hired to write for a particular show, they submit a "packet," a collection of jokes about current events plus some other customized jokes in the format of the particular show.

In this exercise, you're going to create a "packet" of your own to jump-start the Herald. But instead of jokes, you'll be coming up with ideas for projects, as defined in the previous exercise.

First, open your nearest written news source (whether it's the *Guardian*, your local paper's website, or *Dog Fancier Monthly*) and write down the top five headlines.

Set a timer for five minutes. In the allotted time, write five potential project ideas riffing off each headline, for a total of twenty-five ideas. They can be for whatever kind of work you want (short stories, essays, poetry, dramatic script, or something else), and they don't have to all be for the same kind—you don't have to specify. You can apply today's headlines to historical fiction, fantasy, sci fi, magical realism—whatever genres interest you.

Don't think, just write whatever first pops into your head—time is short!

Here's an example:

Headline from Yahoo! News: **Texas Officials Under Scrutiny for Biker Shootout Case**

IDEA #1: "Magic the Gathering" rival gangs turn violent, paper cuts everywhere

IDEA #2: Bikers go to Afghanistan

IDEA #3: Biker gangs vs. drug gangs

IDEA #4: Sentient bikes

IDEA #5: Texas governor gets Harley

When the five minutes are up, see how many ideas you were able to come up with in that tight time frame.

Now open up a different news source and do the same thing again. (This time, you know what five minutes feels like, so you might adjust your own timing accordingly.)

When you're done, take a look at the ideas you generated. Out of these, which might you want to pursue further? Which do you think are terrible? What patterns do you notice?

Put a star next to the ones that most interest you and file them with the ones from the previous exercise. Or, if one really calls to you, it may be what you want to develop into the project you focus on throughout this book. If that's the case, you'll get another chance to look at it more closely in the next exercise.

And if nothing else, you can't claim a shortage of ideas!

Leaving Home

Sitting down and starting a new project is the hardest part of the process for some writers. Jessie, a writer I coached, was happy to spend months doing research, making notes, and even putting together an outline, but when it came time to actually write "Chapter One" and keep going from there, she balked. Whenever we talked, she always had reasons to put off the actual writing a little longer—she needed to research an aspect of her subject matter just a bit more, or there was a hole in the outline she needed to address, or this week really wasn't a good time.

I called her out on her hesitation and invited her to dig deeper into what was holding her back. Confronting her reluctance head-on gave her a forum to talk about it, and what she uncovered was fear. She was afraid of what would happen once her ideas came out of her head and onto the page. As long as those ideas remained in her imagination, the project was as brilliant and complex as she envisioned it. Once she actually wrote the words down, though, the manuscript would be what all first drafts are: messy, disordered, with some parts that were just bad and would definitely be cut later and others that didn't fully express what she was trying to say—what Anne Lamott calls "shitty first drafts."

Many myths begin with a reluctant Hero who would prefer to stay at home, knowing the adventure will likely be long, uncomfortable, even dangerous. You might feel this way as a writer: not eager to let this idea actually lead you down the road of committing to working on it, because the writing process, too, can take you far from comfort and safety.

But in the end, writers write. If you want to benefit from all the rewards of the journey, you have to begin by exploring your idea further on the page.

EXERCISE: BEGINNING THE JOURNEY

For this exercise, have a project in mind that you'd like to begin. Set aside twenty minutes.

- What exactly is the idea? Write out a brief description of what the Herald is calling you to create.

- Write five sentences that are *not* the first sentence of this project.

- Write the last line of the project—again, give yourself five options.

- Name five options for characters, one of whom will show up one-third of the way through the piece.

- Write three different paragraphs from the climax.

- Write a full page that takes place about a quarter of the way into the piece.

If you've passed the twenty-minute mark and want to keep going, do. If you run out of time in the middle, set yourself another twenty-minute time slot for tomorrow and pick up where you left off. Keep doing this until you finish the whole exercise.

Now, see if there's anything here that you want to expand further. Eventually, this may become your writing project.

Be the Change

A new idea gives us a forum to study and enhance elements of craft, particularly those areas we may identify as our weaknesses. It's also an opportunity to investigate our own writing process and find ways to make it more effective and more fulfilling. It's a chance to learn, to evolve, to expand: an invitation to change.

The Herald is an agent of change, in our writing and in our lives. When we sense that, like it or not, the clock on the way we were living has run out and we need to boldly stride in a new direction, that's the voice of the Herald.

Some people thrive on change; others avoid it and even fear it. Change can be difficult, complicated, and tends to involve a lot of uncertainty. For this reason, we often avoid making a change, preferring to continue with the status quo even if it's making us suffer.

Psychologist Jeffrey Kottler argues that most people don't undertake a change in their lives unless one of these five conditions occurs: life transitions (like leaving home, hitting a milestone birthday, retiring); straight-up boredom; acknowledgment that something is broken or needs fixing; rewards that make the change seem worthwhile; and crisis, some catastrophic event.

I've seen many coaching clients recognize that the time has come to shift gears in their lives—to quit or switch jobs, to make a geographical move, to break off a romantic relationship—but hesitate so long that eventually, the change comes to them in the form of crisis: layoffs, being forced to move, getting dumped.

When we really need to make a change, though, we often project that need out into the world, sometimes without even realizing we're doing it. Spend enough time in an untenable situation that you have the power to control and, eventually, you'll start seeing your inner thirst for change appearing outside you, poking at you, until you take action.

After a postcollege year of struggling and living with her parents, Maggie landed a job as an assistant at the then-most powerful publicity firm in Hollywood. An art major in college, Maggie was passionate about film, and her new job gave her entrée into the inner circles of the industry. She saw movies before the critics did. She got to hang out with celebrities, and knew which gossip was true and which was fabricated. She traded in the currency of the film world: secrets, movie-set swag, Oscar screener videos. She loved the way that currency elevated her status and her friends' envy of the perceived glamour of her job.

But there was nothing glamorous about spending her weekends doing her boss's ironing, or being asked to fake a famous country singer's signature on a stack of headshots to be given to cancer patients, a task she was deemed qualified to do because "you're an artist, right?" Maggie found herself spending hours writing materials for press junkets, only to have everything remotely interesting cut from the text. She was pouring her talents into a bottomless well that had no real use for them. A small voice inside her kept telling her to get out of there, but the part of her that loved the perks and the cachet, and was afraid of taking a risk in a world where she wouldn't always be the smartest person in the room, kept her hanging on to the job.

One day, Maggie was on the phone with an actor who was starring in a popular TV police drama. A longtime client of the firm's, he'd talked with Maggie a few times before and knew a little about her academic background and interests. As they chatted while he waited for Maggie's boss to take his call, the actor asked Maggie why she wasn't in graduate school. She offered up the same excuses she'd been telling herself—that she wasn't prepared enough, that she was afraid she wouldn't get in, and so on. But the actor wasn't buying it.

"The next time I call," he told Maggie in his good-cop voice, "I don't want you to still be working here."

For months, Maggie had been pushing away the inner voice telling her to make a change. But when that same voice came out of someone she admired and respected—making her feel witnessed and understood—the part of her needing a change was validated and got louder. And the part of her that loved the Hollywood connections, the ego trip, and the swag bags was left with its roots showing.

In that moment, Maggie realized that if she didn't make a change soon, she'd be slowly taken over by the part of herself she liked least, and turn into a person she wouldn't even want to be friends with.

When that actor next called his publicist, Maggie was gone from the firm. She started a graduate art program within the year.

Creating our own change, rather than waiting for it to come to us, gives us a much-needed sense of agency and control in our lives.

Creating our own change, rather than waiting for it to come to us, gives us a much-needed sense of agency and control in our lives. In his book *59 Seconds*, psychologist Richard Wiseman cites researchers Kenneth Sheldon and Sonja Lyubomirsky, who conducted a series of experiments that involved two kinds of participants: those who'd recently experienced "circumstantial change" (change that had been caused by someone else, such as getting a raise) and those in the midst of "intentional change" (change that the participants initiated, like embarking on a new career). The people who initiated their own change maintained happiness for much longer than the others, who experienced a bump in joy that leveled out once the newness of the experience had worn off.

When change is imposed on us, its novelty quickly fades and it becomes part of the fabric of our day-to-day lives. But when we make our own change, we create, in Wiseman's words, "a constantly changing psychological landscape" that continues to excite us and give our days meaning.

Put another way, we mix up the storytelling so the Hero's Journeys of our lives continue to be good entertainment.

This is what we want for our writing and our lives: a landscape that changes, keeping our work fresh, our brains challenged, and our ears always open for the next call of inspiration.

This is what we want for our writing and our lives: a landscape that changes, keeping our work fresh, our brains challenged, and our ears always open for the next call of inspiration.

CHAPTER THREE

allies

build your support system

Can you think of a story—a book, movie, myth, or folktale—in which the Hero makes it through the entire journey, with all its moments of challenge and jubilation, without anyone else's help?

Most writing books focus on what you can do on your own, and don't give much real estate to the people in your life. But having a strong support system is one of the most crucial elements to a healthy writing practice.

In myth, **Allies** are the Hero's friends, the ones who stick by the Hero's side even when the road becomes rocky and the monsters frightening. Allies can lighten a dark mood, help Heroes with difficult tasks, provide solutions to thorny problems that Heroes can't solve on their own, and be cheerleaders who spur Heroes on. When a Hero is tempted toward the dark side or becomes confused or lost, Allies are there to remind the Hero of the core values that have driven the journey and the mission the Hero must fulfill.

By remaining loyal, supportive, and dedicated to the Hero's mission, Allies model for the Hero what these qualities look like, even if everyone else surrounding the Hero is duplicitous or manipulative. Allies give Heroes the chance to experience what true friendship feels like and to practice empathy and even love.

Allies are much more than mere sidekicks or buddies. A Hero's Ally may be the one person in the entire journey who will continue, no matter the peril, to offer the Hero a truthful mirror to look into.

In this chapter, I will give you the tools to consciously clarify who your own Allies are, how they can help you, and how to set them as the foundation of your process. And if you don't already have Allies, not to worry—we'll look at ways to cultivate them. You might discover one where you least expect to.

> *A Hero's Ally may be the one person in the entire journey who will continue, no matter the peril, to offer the Hero a truthful mirror to look into.*

Do not underestimate the importance of Allies. A well-established support system can make the difference between meeting and falling short of your goals. Allies might seem like minor characters, but they are the key to following your own Hero's Journey all the way to the boon you seek.

The Three Core Needs

We can't choose the families we're born into, but we can choose our support systems—the people we count on and trust. We tend to build them out of some combination of family members, romantic partners, and/or friends, plus a few others who don't fall neatly into any of those categories. We look to these people for love and compassion, and generally they look to us to provide the same. If you are very fortunate, you already have family members who love you, a partner who supports and encourages you, and/or friends who cheer you on in your endeavors.

But this doesn't mean you have Allies.

When I asked one of my coaching clients what people in her life supported her in her writing, she told me about her husband, who worked in IT and didn't get "the whole writing thing" but was loving and encouraging; her best friend, a teacher who was willing to check the writer's work for grammatical errors but didn't have much knowledge about creative writing; and a large extended family that was proud of her "hobby" and was convinced she'd be "a famous author just like that woman who wrote Harry Potter" someday.

My client had a life that was rich with love and support, but she didn't have an Ally in her writing process—or she hadn't, until we started working together.

As a coach, I step into my clients' lives in the role of Ally, at least temporarily. Having seen through many writers' eyes what they most crave from Allies, I've been able to summarize those needs into three general categories. These three types of Allies are based on tropes that have appeared in myths across cultures ever since the first stories were told.

THE TWIN

Imagine living your whole life feeling like an outsider. You don't fit into your family; you've never found your social niche; no matter where you go, you just don't quite belong. You have people who love you, but they don't *get* you; they don't see the world the way you do. You feel like Superman, raised on a foreign planet, or a fairy child swapped with a human as an infant.

Now imagine you discover you have a long-lost twin. The quirks, habits, and worldviews you've always been taught are weird are completely normal to this person. Your twin sees things just as you do, and sees you just as you are without trying to change you into someone else.

For writers who don't know any other writers, life can feel isolating. You are consumed with a never-ending task that your loved ones can't really wrap their heads around, and you see yourself through their eyes as a weirdo. I've coached writers who have asked me questions like, "Do other writers ever feel insecure?" and "Sometimes I start writing in the morning and discover that I'm still in my pajamas when my partner comes home—is that normal?" Even when you're having an experience common to writers the world over, you can still feel like the only one who's ever felt that way if you've never known another creative artist.

Like you, other artists feel that inexplicable compulsion to create; like you, they experience moments of exhilaration and crushing self-doubt while to any uninformed observer it looks like they're just sitting in front of a computer. Like you, they're on a Hero's Journey.

Meeting an Ally who's a fellow artist can feel like encountering your identical twin. You've had the same experiences; you see life the same way; you can speak in a shared shorthand that others can't decipher.

Meeting an Ally who's a fellow artist can feel like encountering your identical twin.

Or the ideal Ally for you might be more of a fraternal twin—someone just like you, but with key differences. This Ally's strengths may be your weaknesses, and vice versa; you complement each other.

Being understood makes us feel less alone and brings us clarity in the process.

An Ally who's had her own struggles can more convincingly remind you when you hit a wall in your writing that you're capable of overcoming it. And when your Ally is facing a challenge, cheering him on with empathy and understanding will encourage you, too.

When Leila Sales and Rebecca Serle met at a networking event, they were both struggling writers in their early twenties. Neither had been published, though both dreamed of becoming authors. They hit it off at the happy hour and kept in touch periodically. But their connection was cemented when Leila invited Rebecca to join her on a road trip she was taking to do research for a novel she was working on. Destination: Colonial Williamsburg.

In the hours in the rental car from New York City to Virginia, Leila and Rebecca discovered how much they had in common. They had markedly distinct personalities—Leila could typically be found dancing until sunrise at a warehouse party in an obscure corner of Brooklyn, while Rebecca was more likely to be practicing yoga and meditation at a wellness retreat in the woods. But their approaches to writing were remarkably similar.

They found themselves talking about their characters, Leila told me, "as if they were real people"—gossiping about them, wondering about their motivations and what they would or wouldn't do—even though they'd never read each other's work. Neither had ever had a friend she could talk about her writing with this way before.

The conversation continued, well beyond the trip to Williamsburg, spanning both writers' first novels being published, and second, and third. The two even wrote a novel together. To this day, their kinship remains strong.

This kind of Ally doesn't have to write in the same genre or category as you, share your working style, or have the same goals as you do to understand where you're coming from and what you're going through. Your Ally doesn't even need to be another writer; you might find the person who understands you best is a composer, choreographer, director, or some other kind of creative artist. It can often be refreshing and inspiring to get insights from artists from other spheres. But whatever the differences between you, the twin-like connection you share nourishes your work.

THE WITNESS

One of the hardest aspects of writing is actually sitting down and doing it on a regular basis, especially if you don't have an external deadline. This is one of the most common reasons writers come to me for coaching. Many of the writers I work with seek me out after spending months or years writing on their own and, usually, struggling to stick to a regular schedule and meet their goals in the timeline they want.

If you didn't get something done at your job, your boss would hold you accountable, but if nobody's holding you accountable for meeting your page goal for the day or completing your draft by the end of the year, it can be hard to motivate yourself to hit that target. While we'll continue to explore a variety of ways to keep yourself motivated in the chapters that follow, there's no replacement for the kind of accountability that another person can provide.

This isn't just about putting in the time at the desk. We need another person—an Ally—to share the burden of our dreams, because that will spur us to work toward making those dreams a reality.

In college, DC Pierson was a chronic procrastinator. He often found himself in the computer lab late at night, intending to get schoolwork done but instead writing short fiction he'd post on his blog. He was at his most creative when writing to avoid doing assigned work. This wasn't great for his grade point average, but he did manage to accumulate a large collection of stories online.

Some months after graduating, he was on his way to his first of many sucky temp jobs when he ran into a friend and fellow writer on the subway. She said she really liked what she'd read on his blog.

"You should write a novel," she told him.

DC had never seriously considered writing a novel; he hadn't gotten much further than fantasizing about having written one. "Yeah, I want to someday," he replied without much thought.

His friend's smiling face became stern. "You know," she told him, "a lot of people say they want to write a novel someday, but not a lot actually do it."

After their conversation, DC continued on his way to the office, but his friend's words stuck with him. When he got to his desk, he wrote her an email. *I really do want to write a novel*, he told her with a fervor he hadn't felt before. *But to do it, I need your help.*

He asked her to do the following: Every time they saw each other, she was to ask him if he had started the book yet, how it was going, and basically harangue him about it until his answers changed. She agreed.

Though they only ran into each other a few times over the coming months, just knowing someone else was out there holding him accountable was enough motivation for DC. He finished his first novel, *The Boy Who Couldn't Sleep and Never Had To*, within a year. Three years after the subway encounter with his friend, DC was a published author.

An Ally who holds you accountable is an unbiased witness to your actions. This Ally isn't there to judge you, to pressure you or push an

the hero is you

agenda on you. His or her job is simply to hold an awareness of the work you have set out to do and the work you actually do.

Accountability works differently for everyone. I've coached writers who would email me every evening to tell me what they got done that day, almost like a journal, and others for whom just knowing I was out there and aware of their goals was enough to motivate them. Some writers send me weekly updates on their progress; others prefer to discuss their progress in our sessions.

You may have already asked a loved one—a partner, a friend, a family member—to hold you to your goals, and that may be working well for you. I find this can sometimes be dicey, because loved ones aren't unbiased and do tend to have an agenda, even if it's a supportive one. Making them your witness can create friction and upset the power dynamic in the relationship. But an Ally who provides accountability without emotional involvement can quietly motivate without stirring up any tension or resentment. Plus, you don't have to see them every day.

Providing accountability doesn't require a deep relationship or huge commitment. The person can be on the other side of the globe, a stranger you met in an online writing forum, or someone who isn't a writer at all. I know one writer who likes to meet up with a friend who's studying for medical school. They work across the table from one another at a coffee shop, neither really understanding what the other is doing, but providing to one another an Ally who knows when the work is getting done.

You can go out and find an accountability partner, or you can invite them to you. Author Carol Goodman lives in a house in New York's Hudson Valley full of cozy nooks that are perfect for working. When she's revising, she often invites friends—writers or not—to join her. Her stepdaughter is sometimes there, too, researching her PhD thesis, so the house will be filled with silently industrious colleagues, each tucked into his or her own room pecking away at a laptop, taking breaks together to share lunch and compare notes before returning to the project at hand.

Carol told me these sessions are like "a game of writing chicken." Whenever she gets tired or wants to stop, she listens to the tapping of the keyboard in the next room and thinks, *Well, I'm not going to be the first one to quit!*

An Ally who is your partner in accountability bears witness to your work in a way that motivates you to keep going.

THE SOOTHSAYER

We don't demand unflinching honesty from everybody in our lives. When we ask a loved one "Does this make me look fat?" for example, we tend to want affirmation and validation, not bald feedback. Naturally, healthy relationships involve plenty of honest communication—most of us wouldn't trust someone who endlessly, insincerely praised us. But there are times when our greatest need is to be loved without critique or reservation. And often, even when we ask our loved ones to be brutally honest, they simply don't have the objectivity to see us with a sufficiently critical eye.

> *Allies, though, like soothsayers out of myth, can tell us the truth, even when it stings.*

Allies, though, like soothsayers out of myth, can tell us the truth, even when it stings. Whether they're calling us out about our writing on the page, our behavior in our practice, or whatever else their keen eyes take in, good Allies are gifted with the ability to be kindly, constructively honest.

Certainly, teachers, agents, and editors can tell us the truth about our work. But we don't always have access to them. And having a peer provide this perspective prepares you for the often much tougher judgment of such professionals. An Ally is the best first reader of your work and honest observer of your process.

Author Rick Moody told me about a novel he began writing in the 1990s, in the wake of his great success with *The Ice Storm*. He quickly penned a hundred pages in the first person, in an almost stream-of-

the hero is you

consciousness style. Before he got any further, he found himself on a train with his friend, writer Jo Ann Beard, and shared a few of the pages with her. "I could sense her exasperation with the haste," he said, "and the seat-of-the-pants approach." Rick knew Jo Ann well enough to be able to read her reaction instantly, before she even put her feedback into words.

When he got home, he looked at the whole hundred pages and threw away ninety-six of them. With the four pages that remained, he ditched the first person, changed the perspective, and slowed down his process, taking a more thoughtful pace. In this new way, he wrote a fifth page, and a sixth, and kept going.

The book became *Purple America*, and it's still among the novels he takes the most pride in. He'd had to write those ninety-six pages, even though he ended up throwing them away, to get where he was ultimately going. But it had taken an Ally—one who offered Rick her unvarnished, instinctual response to the work—to give him the push he needed.

We need these soothsaying Allies to tell us what they really think about our new chapters or our latest idea for how to fix the ending. When we get lost in the process and can't remember our vision for a project or our mission as writers, these Allies are the ones who remind us who we really are, at the heart of it all. And with their honesty, they challenge us to become even better versions of ourselves, not only as writers but as people.

Mallory Ortberg and Nicole Cliffe first connected when Nicole was the coeditor of *The Hairpin*, a blog Mallory wrote for. Since they lived in different cities, they didn't actually meet in person until after they'd been friends for nearly a year—but in that time, they'd grown so close that when Mallory finally went to Utah to visit Nicole, she told me, "we ran into each other's arms" at the airport. With perfectly matched ways of thinking and complementary skill sets, the two knew from the beginning they were destined to work together, and they ended up founding and editing their own blog, *The Toast*, not long after that Utah meeting.

Mallory told me that when the women went into business together, they agreed on one rule: they were not allowed to complain about each other to anyone but one another. If one had a problem with something the other was doing, she had to trust her business partner enough to give her the criticism directly.

This rule became an anchor throughout their working relationship, which involved many different kinds of collaboration, from the business to the creative. It forced them to have conversations that they might otherwise have shied away from.

One day, Nicole came up with a concept for a funny piece for her and Mallory to write together. She created the shell of the piece, outlining it briefly with bullet points, and sent it over to Mallory. Mallory fleshed it out and thought it was hilarious. Normally, she'd have then passed it back to Nicole to edit, but she impetuously published it to the blog instead.

Right after the post went live, Mallory's phone rang.

Nicole told Mallory she was surprised that she'd bulldozed ahead with the piece. Hurt, Nicole said that leaving her out made her feel like a worker bee—like she'd just created a format for Mallory to be funny in, rather than the two of them creating humor together.

Mallory's first impulse was to be defensive—make excuses, chalk her behavior up to carelessness, find a way to turn it around and blame Nicole. But the truth was, she'd known exactly what she was doing. Mallory told me she'd noticed herself developing a habit of using the fact that she was a creative, artistic person to get people to excuse her "carelessness" when she consciously overstepped or took advantage.

But Nicole wouldn't fall for that. She knew Mallory too well, and she was too committed to preserving honesty in their relationship.

So instead of finding a way to twist the situation, Mallory apologized, and they moved forward. She still returns to that moment as a reminder that if Nicole thought highly enough of her to believe she could rise above her own excuses, she can and should see herself that way, too.

A soothsaying Ally isn't only honest with us, but challenges us to be more honest with ourselves. With the help of such an Ally, we can develop into more evolved Heroes.

Assessing Your Allies

You won't necessarily find twin-like understanding, a witness in accountability, and a truth-telling soothsayer all in one person. In fact, you may not *want* them that way. If you have an Ally who provides you with compassion and understanding, you might prefer to get the judgment of the soothsayer from other quarters. Sometimes, the best witness is someone who hasn't read your work at all, allowing that person to provide accountability with even less of an agenda.

Whether they all show up in one ideal writing partner or you seek them out from different people in your lives, each type represents a core need that Allies can fulfill for you. So let's find out which of these needs are being met in your life—or who might be able to meet them.

EXERCISE: YOUR CORE NEEDS

Think of five moments from your writing life in the past several months. They don't have to be big turning points, just snapshots of your life as a writer. They could focus on the creative (a breakthrough about a plot problem, a day when you were really on fire, a decision about how to incorporate some feedback) or the more personal (a conversation about your writing career).

Describe each moment, one sentence per moment, including who (if anyone) was a part of each moment with you.

Write all the names of the people from these moments in a list. Who from your life has played a key role in your writing this year? Who supported your writing and who showed up as a source of conflict for you? Is there anybody major missing from this list?

Now, use the list of people to take the following quiz. Each time a statement is true for a person, put the appropriate sign next to her or his name. You can put the sign next to as many names as the statement applies to.

II

Put a twin symbol next to . . .

1. This person and I have a lot in common as writers.

2. Sometimes, this person can articulate what I'm trying to say even better than I can.

3. I can go to this person for advice when I'm struggling with my process.

4. When this person talks about the writing process, I hear so many things that resonate with my own experiences.

5. Sometimes I feel like this person and I are walking on parallel paths.

Put a witness symbol next to . . .

6. This person is at least as dedicated and motivated as I am.

7. This person is also working toward a major goal, just like me.

8. This person always shows up to appointments on time and sticks to plans.

9. If I had to leave my pet with someone for two weeks, I'd leave it with this person.

10. This person has completed several projects he/she started.

Put a soothsayer symbol next to . . .

11. I can trust this person to always tell me when something in my writing isn't working.

12. This person doesn't let me get away with any excuses.

13. I can't lie to this person.

14. No matter how tough the criticism, this person has my best interests at heart.

15. When I step up to the challenges this person offers me, I grow as a person.

Now you can see how fully the people in your writing life are serving the three core needs we identified in this chapter.

The more twin icons appear beside a name, the more you feel that person understands you. The more witness icons appear beside a name, the more you believe you can rely on that individual for accountability. And the more soothsayer icons are next to someone's name, the more honest you feel that person is with you.

Notice whether these people are very discrete or if all the qualities land with one or several of the people on the list. Take note if you have people on your list with no signs next to their names, though this doesn't suggest they are not valuable people in your life in other ways.

Cultivating Allies

It's my hope that you came out of the last exercise with a roster of pretty strong Ally candidates. But what if you discovered that you don't currently have people in your life meeting one, or all three, of the needs we identified? How do you find Allies?

As you've seen from the stories in this chapter, Allies can come into your life in many ways. You can meet them by accident or seek them out, find them at places where artists gather or run across them in the course of your ordinary life. A potential Ally could already be your neighbor, your colleague, a friend-of-a-friend.

The most likely way to find an Ally who can meet your needs is by being a Hero: by serving your work and following your mission.

A few years after moving to New York, Adam Wade was having a hard time. He'd left New Hampshire and braved the most roach-filled, gloom-infused New Jersey basement apartments to pursue his dream of performing as a professional storyteller, but found himself still struggling to make ends meet.

But every month, he went to the Moth, a live storytelling show. Anybody could perform in the Moth; all you had to do was get to the venue early enough to make the cut.

One evening, as Adam stood in line outside the theater hoping to be able to try out his latest story, he struck up a conversation with Keesha, who'd recently moved to New York. Adam found her bright and funny, sweet and easy even for a shy guy to talk to, and she seemed to enjoy his company, too.

So they decided to do the most intimate thing two people can do: share their writing with each other.

Adam and Keesha started to meet up the week after the Moth Story-SLAM to share the new stories they wanted to bring to the next show. With more of a writing background than Adam had, Keesha gave Adam the kind of criticism he couldn't get from other performers, and he offered her a helpful perspective on how to better bring her stories to life onstage. But what Adam appreciated most about Keesha was that she called him out on his bullshit. Nursing a minor crush on his writing partner, Adam yearned to impress her, but the harder he tried, the more she cut him down. "You're acting too writerly," she'd tell him; over and over, she pushed him to be true to his own voice instead of trying to be someone he wasn't.

Keesha taught Adam a valuable lesson: try to impress your audience, and you'll lose them. Instead, she emphasized, focus on making a genuine connection. This wasn't something he could learn from recording himself onstage and listening to it after the show; it was a gift only another person could give him.

Although Adam and Keesha eventually drifted apart, he told me he still hears her voice in his head when he's editing his own work. Her influence as his Ally left a lasting impression.

The best way to find an Ally is to be an Ally. Adam and Keesha were both looking for help, and both got satisfaction from helping another writer. When you are in your darkest hour, you may feel like you have nothing to teach or contribute, but you might have exactly what someone else desperately needs. By helping that writer, you gain confidence in your work and in yourself.

The best way to find an Ally is to be an Ally.

You are the Hero in your own journey, but you are an Ally in someone else's.

A writer's job is to cultivate empathy, in an ongoing quest to better understand human beings and why we do the things we do. When you apply that empathy to your life, you discover that the world around you is full of people who need *your* understanding, *your* objectivity, and *your* honesty.

You have the power to inspire your Allies to create the best work of their lives. And you and your work will benefit immeasurably from the experience.

CHAPTER FOUR

the mentor

learn from all teachers and
follow your inner wisdom

What's the best writing advice you've ever gotten?

When I posed this question to several writers across various disciplines, the advice they offered up wasn't especially groundbreaking: "write long," "avoid whimsy," "explore your weird obsessions," and so on. Much more interesting than the advice itself, though, were the characters behind it—the older, more experienced writers, editors, and teachers who'd said these words that had stuck in the heads of their recipients for years or even decades. The writers described these advice-givers vividly, with deep affection and appreciation. Even if the advice didn't dazzle me with its profundity, it had clearly helped these writers.

Maybe the brilliance wasn't in the words, but in the people who said them. These writers were remembering the impact of good **Mentors** on their work and on their lives.

In myth, Mentors are older characters who'd already traveled their own journeys and convey the wisdom they've learned to younger Heroes. Mentors teach, protect, and bestow gifts on Heroes to help them on the road ahead.

Mentors teach, protect, and bestow gifts on Heroes to help them on the road ahead.

The title "Mentor" comes from the name of a character in Homer's *Odyssey* who appeared as an old man to Odysseus's son and helped the boy on his journey to find his lost father. But Mentor was actually the goddess Athena in disguise, and good Mentors in stories can often hold a kind of magical power for the Heroes they help—as long as these mentees do the work required to earn their generous aid.

Writers often seek Mentors in the form of teachers or professors, or successful, established authors. Writing sometimes feels like reinventing the wheel, and it can be incredibly helpful to speak with someone who's already been through what you're going through and can give you perspective and guidance. The advice of a great teacher can stick with you for life and become a part of you and your process.

> *The advice of a great teacher can stick with you for life and become a part of you and your process.*

However, when good Mentors don't appear organically in your life, chasing after them can be a fruitless endeavor. Worse still, bad Mentors can do real damage to your work and your psyche. As Sheryl Sandberg discusses in *Lean In*, focusing on looking for a Mentor rather than on developing your strengths can refract your priorities and encourage dependency on others.

I've seen coaching clients become so focused on the idea of finding the perfect Mentor that this search becomes an excuse to put their progress in permanent suspended animation.

So often, what we are looking for in this wise, knowledgeable other, we can find in ourselves. You don't need a Mentor to teach you, protect you, and give you gifts. You already possess a source of inner wisdom that can funnel knowledge to you, guide you through the hazards of the writing process, and connect you with the tools you need to find your way on the journey.

You can be your own Mentor. This chapter will show you how. And it'll also give you the tools to recognize a great Mentor if such a person comes into your life.

Teachers Versus Mentors

Mentoring yourself begins with identifying what a good Mentor is—and isn't.

Playwright Kyoung Park had encountered all kinds of teachers in his academic career—some brilliant and helpful, some only the former, and some neither, including a memorable professor who refused to offer students any feedback in a semester-long writing workshop. Kyoung had learned something from all of them—but none had been mentors.

By the time Kyoung was introduced to director Lee Breuer through his graduate program, he was pretty self-sufficient. But the mentorship was part of the offerings of the program, so he was willing to take advantage of it. Little did Kyoung know he'd just begun what became, in his words, "one of the most successful mentorship partnerships" that the students of his class had with professionals in the theater world.

Lee and Kyoung instantly clicked, and there was little the older man wouldn't do for his mentee. While some other mentors did "the bare miminum," Lee helped Kyoung write and direct his show and find the proper venue to produce it, facilitating Kyoung's big break in the theater world three years after he'd graduated. Well after completing the program, Kyoung worked for Lee as his assistant director, dramaturge, and company/production/stage manager. Though they no longer work together, he will always consider Lee a mentor who "forever changed the way I do what I do."

What have you learned from the best teachers you've had? From the worst? What lessons from each do you still carry with you? What old lessons might you have forgotten that could serve you now?

In *The Power of Myth*, Joseph Campbell makes a distinction between Eastern and Western Mentors, explaining that the Eastern tradition features gurus who guide their acolytes on a spiritual path similar to their own, whereas in the West, uniqueness and individuality are placed in the highest esteem. Which paradigm resonates more with you? Do you like the idea of following in the footsteps of someone who's already traveled the road or bushwhacking your own route with a Mentor's encouragement?

Within and beyond these two paradigms lies a multitude of different ways to teach, to guide, and to be a Mentor. Part of Mentoring yourself means recognizing the methods that work best for you, so you can use them to access the wisdom you already possess.

EXERCISE: REMEMBERING MENTORS

Think about a favorite teacher or Mentor you've had in your life. The person could be an academic or artistic teacher, librarian, athletic coach, college professor, boss or manager, or anyone who mentored you, even a parent or other relative. If you can't think of anyone who's played this role in your life, think about a famous person you admire whose advice you respect or the author of your favorite book.

Like the writers at the beginning of the chapter, write down one or two pieces of advice this person gave you that you still remember.

What were the qualities that made this person such a good Mentor? List them.

Notice how this Mentor helped you and what made this person a valued Mentor for you. We'll use this information later in the chapter as we continue to build a picture of the ideal Mentor you can be to yourself.

Teachers as Lighthouses

One of the tricky aspects of the student-teacher relationship—and this is true for any Mentor-mentee relationship—is the power dynamic. We seek out Mentors who are older, more experienced, know more than we do, because we want to benefit from everything they've learned. Often, they are people we greatly admire, whether because of their accomplishments, their personalities, or both. Great teachers are often charismatic; we love being around them and yearn for their praise and approval.

There's nothing wrong with this until it begins to put your autonomy in jeopardy. Your job as a Hero is to remain focused on everything you are protecting and serving on your journey: your mission as a writer, the goals you're working toward, your gifts. A Mentor can advise you, but at the end of the day, you are the one with your best interests at heart—for your project and yourself—and you're the one who knows what you need.

When students hand their Mentors the reins to their own work or lives, they're giving up their power. I got to witness this firsthand when I studied under writing guru Julia Cameron.

Before the end of the first day of class, I was already rolling my eyes. Not at Cameron—it was fascinating to see the author of *The Artist's Way* in action. No, my eyeball gymnastics were inspired by the army of acolytes I found myself seated among.

Cameron was outlining her expectations for us, which were essentially the same as those set up in *The Artist's Way*: write "Morning Pages" and go on a weekly "Artist's Date." Given the fannish adoration emanating from the majority of the class, it seemed a given that everybody present had read *The Artist's Way*. Several of the students had even taken previous classes with Cameron. When she explained the concept of Morning Pages (write three stream-of-consciousness pages every morning when you wake up), several hands shot up.

"Can I take a shower first?"

"What if I can't function until I've had my coffee?"

"May I pee before I write?"

This was when I began reflexively examining the upper reaches of my eyelids.

Cameron, who'd clearly been facing this barrage of earnest queries for decades, said, "I'll tell you what I tell all my classes: I teach adults."

With her response, Cameron highlighted exactly what struck me as so odd about these questions: their childishness. *Surely,* I thought, *these educated adults don't really believe they need someone to tell them when to shower, when to urinate, and when to write.* But the students were giving Cameron totemic power, imbuing her advice with significance beyond its actual meaning, in their hope that the right combination of magical words would be the charm to unlock some hitherto unknown talent or creativity.

By putting Cameron on this pedestal, they were actually bringing themselves lower. By empowering her, they were disempowering themselves, becoming infantilized down to their most basic body functions like actual babies. The more heavily these students relied on their faith in the mystical power of Cameron's guidance to carry them, the less able they were to walk on their own and do the work of being writers.

I stepped out of class that day more certain than ever that I would bow down at the altar of no Mentor. Cameron and her teachings bore wisdom, and over the duration of the class, I would do my best to extract as much of that wisdom as I could. But I would never do so at the expense of my own power.

A good Mentor may be divinely inspiring, but isn't actually a goddess in a human disguise. Years ago, as a teenager with dreams of becoming a famous writer, I sought audience with David Mamet while he was shooting a film on location near my hometown. When I boldly knocked on the door of his trailer, he answered, barefoot and brushing his teeth. He didn't offer me any timelessly valuable writing advice between spit and rinse, but we did have a long conversation about the college application process because his daughter, Zosia, and I were both in the thick of it. Famous writers: they're just like us!

In an ideal Mentor-mentee dynamic, there is no pedestal, no mountain for the wise to perch on. The relationship should be built on mutual respect that acknowledges what both Mentor and mentee have to teach one another, and that recognizes each person as coming from a place of strength.

As Campbell says in *The Power of Myth*, "Different teachers may suggest exercises, but they may not be the ones to work for you. All a teacher can do is suggest. He is like a lighthouse that says, 'There are rocks over here, steer clear. There is a channel, however, out there.'" (That applies to this book as well, by the way.)

The ultimate authority you must answer to isn't your Mentor; it's yourself.

The ultimate authority you must answer to isn't your Mentor; it's yourself.

the hero is you

Your Mentor isn't the one whose name will appear under the title of your project; you are. Your Mentor doesn't have to live with you every day until death; you do.

Now let's connect with that place of strength in you to discover what Mentor wisdom you already possess.

Inner Mentor

Each of us is guided by a source of inner wisdom, a deeper part of ourselves that knows things our rational mind takes longer to process. I think of it as intuition, but I know that term can sometimes confuse more than it illuminates. Joseph Campbell called it "following your bliss." Some people identify this voice of wisdom as coming from a deity, a beloved deceased person, or an inner Wise Man or Wise Woman. You could also call it instinct or your gut, as it tends to stem from somewhere behind the belly button.

If you're of a more scientific bent, you might call it your "second brain." The neural network lining our alimentary canal contains about a hundred million neurons, a volume second only to the brain itself. While humans probably evolved this complex network so our guts could perform digestion actions without getting the brain involved, there is no question that the "second brain" is connected with our emotions—just notice the butterflies, knot, or brick in your belly the next time you feel excitement, anxiety, or dread. Scientists in the emerging field of neuro-gastroenterology are still exploring just how much the brain in our gut knows and what it does for us.

Whatever or whomever you ascribe that voice to, it's the part of yourself that tells you whether your actions are in alignment with what's true to you. It's what lets us know when something doesn't feel quite right though rationally everything seems fine, or leads us in a new direction even if we're not sure exactly why. Whether you're making a tough decision, sorting through your feelings about a fraught situation, or responding to the creative impulse, this inner wisdom can guide you to make the choice that most deeply resonates with who you are and what you need. No matter if we feel attuned to it or not, we rely on this deeper part of ourselves to guide our actions.

Writing itself is a process of making a million tiny decisions. If you want to totally paralyze yourself, think about the fact that every sentence you write, every word, represents a fork in the road at which you've chosen one path at the expense of thousands of other possible routes. I could've written that last sentence a near-infinite number of ways—using different words, constructing it in a different order, going for a different tone, putting it later in the paragraph, and so on. Every letter we mark on the page is the result of a decision. This is why the invention of the delete key is both the best and worst thing to happen to writers in the twentieth century.

When nonfiction author Cari Lynn embarked on her first work of fiction, she had no idea how paralyzing all those decisions would be. She loved doing the research for her historical novel, but got stuck every time she tried to write a chapter. A simple scene set in a character's office would unleash a barrage of questions: *What would be in an office in 1898? Maybe books—but what books had been published at that time? Whose office is this? Why are we in an office anyway? But where else could this scene take place?*

"It was like a maze," Cari told me. "I'd turn a corner only to find another corner . . . I was caught in this labyrinth that I was creating."

Her turning point came when she finally threw up her hands and decided she didn't have to know all the details in order to write the story. She pushed forward through the first draft, focusing on the plot and characters rather than the historical details. Once she had made the bigger craft decisions, she could go back in revision and make some of those smaller, period-related choices. The important story choices suddenly felt a lot easier, and more intuitive, without all those other questions cluttering up her process.

When you write, your inner Mentor is already in the driver's seat much of the time, guiding the micro-decisions that, letter by letter and word by word, build a piece of writing. If your conscious, buzzy mind didn't scoot over and let a deeper part of yourself drive, you might never get anything done.

We use this internal resource all the time, and tend to do so unconsciously on a sentence-by-sentence level. But when it comes to making bigger decisions—from addressing plot and character questions in our work to how to shape our process to picking a direction at life's many junctures—we need to be able to tap into that source of wisdom more directly.

If your conscious, buzzy mind didn't scoot over and let a deeper part of yourself drive, you might never get anything done.

We're going to strengthen the connection between you and your inner Mentor so you can more actively draw on it for the kind of help Heroes get from their Mentors—protection, teaching, and valuable gifts.

EXERCISE: NAMING YOUR MENTOR

Think about a moment in the past when you were faced with a difficult decision or a thorny question, something you had to resolve on your own.

Write a poem in three parts.

In part one, describe the situation. Use of metaphor is encouraged—you can be as literal or as opaque as you wish.

In part two, remember the voice that arose within you with an answer or a direction. Give that voice an identity. (Some options: a real person, a person from fiction, a god or goddess from mythology, an animal, an element of nature, something you totally make up . . .) Make sure to include the words it said to you.

In part three, portray how you responded to this voice of wisdom: Did you heed it? Did you do the opposite of what it said? What were the results?

For example: I had one of my clients do this exercise when she was facing a difficult decision. She had told me many times that the last time she'd been faced with a decision this major and difficult had been when she was trying to choose where to go to college, so I encouraged her to write about that. In part I of her poem, she portrayed herself as drowning in a sea of the future. In part II, she described a Great Blue Whale appearing, full of ancient wisdom, telling her not to go to college. In part III of the poem, she talked about sinking beneath the surface and floating underwater until the tide carried her to shore—a metaphor for what it felt like to ignore her intuition, go to a school where she was unhappy, and ride out the experience until she eventually found her community and a place for herself.

These were the images and language that resonated with her. Use whatever imagery, vocabulary, and emotions speak to your own experience.

After you've written the poem, notice how you personified your inner voice of wisdom.

If you haven't already, give this Mentor a name. We'll be drawing on this character again later in the chapter.

Asking Questions

I encourage writers to personify their inner Mentors because it helps make that voice feel less elusive. Even though it guides us through many decisions each day, trying to tap into it actively can often feel like being at the doctor's office when the nurse can't find your vein.

Adelaide was floundering when it came to decision-making. She had many desires—to write on a regular basis, to get published, to work on self-improvement—but these ideas all felt vague and amorphous and she had a hard time translating them into decisive action. With a few different projects underway, she had a habit of dabbling without making significant movement on any of them. She'd commit to a specific goal and structure in one coaching session, only to show up at the next with some different goal that was now more important.

When I pressed her about this unwillingness to commit, she said she felt like a feather on the wind, subject to whatever the most recent thought or feeling was that blew through her. She couldn't identify what was truly important to her because each idea or belief seemed, at the moment she conceived of it, to be the most important.

the hero is you

I asked her if there were a deeper, sager voice in her that could cut through these whims and clarify what her true priorities were. She said she felt like she'd been yearning her whole life of fifty-odd years to hear her own inner voice, but that it was always drowned out by her fear of it being wrong.

"Let's see if we can quiet that fear and hear what your inner voice has to say," I told her.

We brought our discussion to a halt, and I asked her to close her eyes and breathe deeply. I walked her through a guided visualization that had her meet the personification of her Mentor, as in the previous exercise, and ask that deeper, wiser part of herself for advice. When she emerged, she was smiling, and her eyes shone with tears.

In the visualization, her Mentor had asked her: *Who are you?*

This question had struck a chord in Adelaide. To her, it meant that she'd been jumping on whatever idea floated her way because she didn't have a clear sense of the motivation beneath her writing. *What do I want to say with my writing? Why is publication important to me?* She hadn't answered these questions, but connecting with her Mentor revealed their significance to her.

Throughout our time together, Adelaide had been very focused on the idea of "working on" herself. When she asked her Mentor how to proceed, though, she discovered that this "work" had been driven by the question, *What's wrong with me?* The question her Mentor replaced this with was, *Which parts of myself need to be loved today?*

Adelaide has always been afraid the voice within her would be wrong. But when she'd finally really listened to it, it hadn't told her what to do or given her advice—it had simply asked questions. Those questions taught her the importance of clarifying her motivation, showed her a path to being less judgmental and more kind to herself, and gave her a source of wisdom and self-guidance she could finally, after all these years, access.

"This is the path I came in to do," she told me, "the path of finding the way to my center."

In the weeks that followed, these questions guided Adelaide toward settling on a project to focus on and identifying a concrete publication goal. When she stopped trying to fix what was wrong with her and started honoring the aspects of herself that needed attention, she found that the personal development work she'd been pushing herself to do went deeper than it ever had before.

And the next time she was floundering, she had a resource she could go to, if not for answers, then for the gift of questions to guide her.

Lifelines to Your Mentor

Adelaide's fear of being wrong had prevented her from listening to her own wisdom. But after our session, I wondered what she'd done in the past to try and hear it. Sometimes, simply giving our need for clarity a little attention can work surprisingly quickly to raise the volume of our inner wisdom's voice.

If you find yourself in a situation like Adelaide's—struggling with making a decision, unclear about your priorities, or just having a difficult time slicing through the noise to hear what's really true in you—try one or a combination of the techniques below.

FIRST RESPONSE

When I ask my clients big questions, I often follow them up with, "Don't think, just tell me the first thing that pops into your head." Often, your initial, gut response to something—a question, a statement, an idea—is your truest response, before your rational mind has a chance to start constructing arguments. Don't dismiss those arguments but pay attention to your initial reaction.

LISTEN TO THE BODY

We often treat our minds and bodies as if they are separate entities, but they're one cohesive whole. Our bodies are far more than just vehicles to

the hero is you

drive our brains around, and they are often full of emotional signals, like those gut neurons showing us what excites or frightens us. When we ignore those signals, they don't just go away; they may get more extreme until we finally pay attention.

Sally couldn't understand why she kept catching colds. She worked from home, so she wasn't exposed to a lot of germs. She ate a balanced diet, exercised regularly, and had never been bothered by a particularly weak immune system. But for the past year or so, it seemed like she'd caught every little bug that came along.

When I suggested stress might be a factor, Sally pooh-poohed the idea. But when she traced back the timeline, she admitted that the chain of colds had started when she'd taken on a freelance client who gave her lucrative work but terrorized her with aggressive emails and phone calls at odd hours and treated her with utter disrespect. She'd talked herself into the idea that the anxiety was worth the money, but her body wasn't convinced.

Once she started paying more attention to her body's reactions, she noticed that every time she opened her work email, her shoulders tensed, as if bracing herself for the client's latest onslaught. When she was on the phone with the client, she caught herself pulling her arms close to her body, like a boxer, in a protective pose. Her body was telling her this relationship was unhealthy and dangerous.

Even when she recognized all this, she was reluctant to break it off with the client—she believed she needed to "tough it out." When her contract ended, though, her colds stopped. The next time the client approached her with a project, she turned it down.

If you're not sure how you feel about a given situation, notice how your body reacts to it. Your inner wisdom, via your physical responses, may tell you what your conscious mind doesn't want to admit.

CHECKING IN

Set aside ten minutes out of your day to check in with yourself in whatever way works best for you. This could mean writing in a journal, meditating, taking a walk, or simply sitting still—unplugged from the pings and notifications that take us further from our center—and letting yourself think your thoughts. (And when I say unplugged, I mean turn your phone *off!*)

One of my coaching clients makes it a habit to take ten minutes right before our appointments to just sit quietly and connect with herself. Sometimes she only manages one or two minutes, or comes to our call out of breath from running to make it in time. But when she does find ten minutes to focus beforehand, she's more centered, less frazzled, and more able to tap into what she's feeling at gut level rather than just what her busy mind is telling her.

You don't have to make this a rigorous routine that you do every day, although you may, if that's helpful to you. But in a busy life, it's surprisingly easy to forget this simple yet effective tool that's at our disposal whenever we need it.

QUESTIONS

Adelaide's Mentor helped her by asking her questions that resonated. Rather than seeking advice or words of wisdom, observe what questions rise up when you focus on that inner voice. What is your Mentor asking you?

PLAY THE MENTOR ROLE

Imagine someone is coming to you for advice or help. If you were their Mentor, what would you say to them? What advice would you give?

Listening to the Mentor in you means empowering yourself to be a Mentor to others. Think about the qualities you listed in the first exercise. How would you embody these qualities to help someone else? How can you turn that aid around and apply it to your own dilemma?

the hero is you

ASK ALLIES FOR HELP

When you're relying on yourself for Mentoring, it's especially important to have good Allies who can provide some of the support, encouragement, and advice that a Mentor might.

Often, the easiest way to discover what your inner Mentor wants you to know is by talking with someone else. An Ally can be a sounding board, asking you questions and mirroring back the emotions you're expressing both consciously, through what you tell them, and subconsciously, through your body language and what you're leaving unsaid. Often, I don't realize I feel a certain way until I hear it come out of my mouth. Once it's said, you can move past investigating your feelings and into how to take action.

TRUST YOURSELF

The crucial first step to drawing wisdom from your inner Mentor is the willingness to trust yourself. This means empowering yourself to be a source of knowledge and guidance, and believing in your own innate ability to sense what is best for you and your work.

Mentor as a Tool for Structure

Writers often come to me when they're trying to decide whether or not they should enroll in an MFA program. Many considering this option see its biggest appeal as the structure it would impose on them—the deadlines, accountability, and regular feedback that come from being in an organized program.

There are plenty of good reasons to pursue a master's degree. If it's only the structure you're looking for, though, you can create that yourself.

The exercise below is a suggested method for structuring your writing process. Like the Hero Map in chapter one, this is a way to organize your writing practice and give it a container to sit in. If this doesn't appeal to you, you'll find other options throughout the book that might resonate with you more. However, if you loved school and miss the rigor of an academic environment, it might be exactly what you need.

EXERCISE: BACK TO SCHOOL

Following the structure of a university course, you will create a schedule to help yourself stick to a regular writing routine like a student sticks to the requirements and timeline of a class.

Below is a suggestion for how to structure your course, but I encourage you to be creative and to customize this based on what you respond well to. What environment feels most inspiring to you and best fits your lifestyle: a vaunted old institution, an open-ended, DIY-style program, a continuing ed program that has you "studying" evenings and weekends? Think about the classes you've taken in your life that had the biggest impact on you. What elements from those can you apply here?

Have fun with it—we rarely get to design our very own, fully customized educational programs!

Syllabus for Writing [title of current project]

PROFESSOR: [name of Mentor from previous exercise]

NUMBER OF WEEKS: [Estimate how long it will take you to reach the goal you set and mapped out in chapter one.]

Required reading: [Fill in titles of books/articles including research for your project, your favorite books about writing, and any other literature that inspires you and helps keep you going.]

Weekly Schedule

LECTURE: Once a week, set aside a block of time for connecting with your Mentor. You can use this time to meditate, do a guided visualization, or write in your journal; whatever you choose, it should be in a quiet place where you can be undisturbed. Focus on the Mentor from the previous exercise and open

the hero is you

yourself up to whatever that voice wants to tell you. You can bring it specific questions, or just spend time with it, waiting to see what it shares with you.

HOMEWORK: This is your writing assignment, and can be any amount of time, any number of days—up to you. However, you should set a specific amount of time and specific number of days and stick with them. If the schedule you have set turns out to be untenable, adjust it and stick with the new one. If you find you could keep going for longer than the allotted time, or discover you're sitting down to write additional days, increase your outlined expectations. Log your hours and days on an "attendance sheet" to ensure you are showing up.

STUDY GROUP: Check in with an Ally or Allies, at least once a week, to let them know how you are doing, ask for any help or support you might need, and offer the same to them.

STUDY BREAK: Once a week, choose a mini-treat to reward yourself for your hard work and for sticking to the course schedule.

Other optional elements to add: Seminar, Office Hours, anything else you can come up with.

Use these guidelines to weave a structure for your writing process that suits your personality and schedule, feels organic and achievable, has built-in fluidity to allow for the unpredictability of life, and offers you regular positive reinforcement.

At the end of the class—when you reach the goal you've set—find a way to celebrate this milestone with a graduation.

A Student of Life

You are your own Mentor—and like any real-life Mentor, you aren't secretly a god or goddess. You have feet of clay. You have much to teach yourself, but the world has infinitely more to teach you if you're willing to listen.

If you see everyone who crosses your path as a teacher, the world will be your classroom.

Take your inner voice of wisdom seriously, but don't let it be the only voice you hear. If you see everyone who crosses your path as a teacher, the world will be your classroom.

"Everyone you will ever meet knows something you don't," said Bill Nye. Every person, every place, every experience has the potential to teach you something of value.

The more you extract this value from the world around you, the more likely you are to find a Mentor with the qualities you identified at the beginning of the chapter.

Alex Baze didn't find his Mentor until he was thirty-seven years old. After being a high school teacher, a sketch comedy performer in Chicago, and a struggling writer/waiter in Los Angeles, he finally got to quit his restaurant job and moved to New York to write on the staff of *Saturday Night Live*'s "Weekend Update." At *SNL*, he found a kindred spirit in Tina Fey, who was then coanchoring "Weekend Update's" satirical news program with Amy Poehler.

Alex had never considered himself a joke-writer, but he'd spent the past six years studiously watching "Weekend Update" and emailing its head writer ten jokes a week, hoping a few would make the cut. In that time, he'd become a kind of scientist of jokes, taking them apart and seeing how they worked. Now that he was on staff, he had to write thirty-five jokes every day, Monday through Friday.

Tina Fey was an even more mathematical joke writer than Alex, he told me. If she got the idea that a certain news story had the potential for a joke in it, she'd approach it from fifty different angles until she found the perfect way to tell it. There was no such thing as "good enough" with Tina—she deconstructed every joke word by word to find the best possible way to reconstruct each one.

When a joke of Alex's didn't work, she'd tell him so—and she'd explain why and show him how to make it better. She taught him the terminology of comedy, a whole lexicon to identify different parts of a joke that helped Alex understand the inner workings of humor. She taught him that the setup is just as important as the punch line, that the last word of the joke is the most crucial, how to eliminate unnecessary details, and how to lead the audience in the right direction to set them up for your punch line.

Under Tina's tutelage, Alex went on to become the producer and head writer of "Weekend Update," and eventually, he left *SNL* to manage the writing staff at *Late Night with Seth Meyers*. To this day, when Alex is having a challenging day of writing comedy, he pulls up a picture of Tina Fey on his computer screen and mentally runs through each joke in her voice. He told me he thinks, *"Let me hear this in Tina's voice and see what's wrong with it, and how I would fix it for her."*

We know more than we think we do. We may run what we know through a mental filter—a respected teacher, a character we've created, a structure we're following—or hone our ears to hear our inner wisdom. But either way, a Mentor lies within us all.

A Mentor lies within us all.

Says Campbell, "Protective power is always and ever present within the sanctuary of the heart . . . one has only to know and trust, and the ageless guardians will appear."

Trust yourself to lead you to the methods, practices, and habits that are most conducive to your writing. Trust yourself to lead you to good Mentors, a variety of teachers who can help you with different needs at different times, in your writing and in your life. Trust yourself to guide you toward choices that will make you healthy, happy, and fulfilled.

Be your own Mentor, and trust that the Mentoring you receive from the world will carry you forward in your journey.

CHAPTER FIVE

threshold guardians

conquer distraction

It's hard to write a book if you can't sit still. But Gary was determined to try.

A blogger on popular science, Gary came to me for coaching because he wanted help focusing on a nonfiction book project. His first challenge was to create time to work on it—his freelancer's lifestyle made for an unpredictable schedule and frequent interruptions. Even when he was able to set a block of his day aside, though, he'd get distracted by some more time-sensitive assignment and start working on that instead. Or he'd struggle through a few sentences of the book, think, *This sucks, what's the point?* and abandon the manuscript again. He often talked about the writers he idolized and how he dreamed of being like them, but couldn't seem to get through the drafting stage.

The irony was, Gary was incredibly prolific. He could dash off a couple blog posts before breakfast and wrote short pieces for a handful of online publications on a regular basis. But that drive seemed to die when he tried to work on his passion project, and self-imposed structures weren't helping. When he'd given himself homework-like assignments, his inner teenager rebelled against authority. He had tried to participate in National Novel Writing Month, thinking the pressure might be motivating; out of the thirty days, he wrote for one.

Even during our coaching sessions over Skype, I could see him struggling with focus. No matter how absorbed he was in our discussion, he couldn't resist the occasional reflexive glance at his phone. Once, he even peeked at his email on the computer while we were talking. (He probably thought he was being sly, but I could see the browser reflected in his glasses.)

One of Gary's primary goals for our time together was to get out of his own head and into a flow state, where he could forget about everything else but the work. But a threshold stood between him and this ideal, and until he conquered its **Threshold Guardians**, he'd remain unable to write.

Flow

Once a Hero has received the call to adventure, marshaled Allies, and internalized training and guidance from the Mentor, he is ready to leave the familiar world of home behind and enter a foreign land. This "magical world" (which may be literally magical or simply a place unfamiliar enough to elicit growth and change from the Hero) is where the bulk of the journey takes place.

But entering the magical world is rarely simple. The boundary between the old world and this new one is a rigorously policed threshold, and the Hero must use whatever she has gleaned from her journey so far—inherent gifts, the help of Allies, teachings from the Mentor—to get past the Threshold Guardians.

Crossing this boundary is the first real test the Hero must undergo, and the Threshold Guardians are often the first antagonists the Hero meets. These unsavory characters do their best to try to keep the Hero out. They frustrate the Hero, but can inevitably be overcome—otherwise, the journey couldn't continue. They provide a kind of litmus test: how the Hero handles them reveals whether she or he truly has the brains, strength, and quick-thinking abilities to succeed on this journey.

For a writer, the "magical world" of one's process is the state of flow. Psychologist Mihaly Csikszentmihalyi coined the term "flow" in his extensive studies of what he called "optimal experience"—the feeling of being so deeply immersed in a passionate pursuit that you forget about your surroundings and allow self-awareness to fall away. Csikszentmihalyi wrote a whole book about it, but the concept of flow requires little explanation to writers. I suspect you know exactly what I'm talking about.

For a writer, the "magical world" of one's process is the state of flow.

In his book *Focus*, social scientist Daniel Goleman reveals that only about 20 percent of people get into a flow state at least once a day—for the rest, it's less frequent. I'd guess the number is significantly higher for writers, but getting there isn't as simple as turning on a switch.

Life is full of distractions that prevent us from concentrating on our work. It's the rare person who's so free of obligation that nothing can ever intrude on his or her writing time. When we finally do sit down unencumbered by the world's demands, we may still find ourselves at war with our own minds. The inner monologue might go something like this:

Okay, time to focus. Did I leave the oven on? I'd better check—nope, it's fine. Good. Time to write. Ugh, why is writing so hard? Quick phone check. Maybe I should send a text to—nope, put the phone down. I wonder what the cover of my book would look like if it ever got published? What was that book with the beautiful cover I saw recently? Let me just Google it . . . oh, while I'm online, quick Facebook check. Three people's birthdays? Better just wish them a fast "hb" while I'm thinking of it. "Quiz: What character from Scandal are you?" Okay, I'll just do that, then get started writing. What's that buzzing—a text! Let me just respond . . .

If any of this rings a bell, you have dealt with Threshold Guardians. The Threshold Guardians of writing are those neurotic habits that glom on to the process like remoras on a shark's pale belly. They stand between you and your flow state and demand to be wrangled. These impediments come in a variety of flavors, but can largely be distilled into three general categories that we'll be exploring here. Inspired by Threshold Guardians from myths, we'll call them the Hydra, Rakshasa, and Troll.

The Threshold Guardians of writing are those neurotic habits that glom on to the process like remoras on a shark's pale belly. They stand between you and your flow state and demand to be wrangled.

You may recognize one, two, or all three of these Guardians as monsters you fight on a regular basis. We'll discuss each category and identify which Guardians are giving you the most trouble right now; look at ways to tackle each one when they come up; and investigate what the Guardians have to teach us. Irritating though they may be, these monsters may actually want to help you. They're just going about it in completely the wrong way.

EXERCISE: QUIZ: HEROES AT THE THRESHOLD

This exercise is designed to help you identify which Threshold Guardian is plaguing you the most right now, though any of them can cause you problems at different times.

Answer the following questions.

1. What do you check most often?
   a. Airfare and deals to places I'd love to visit one day (3)
   b. My To Do list (2)
   c. My phone for texts, calls, and social media notifications (1)
   d. A combination of the above (4)

2. What would you rather spend your day off doing?
   a. Having fun with my friends and family (1)
   b. Getting everything done so I can start the week fresh (2)
   c. Taking it easy (3)
   d. I have a very specific idea of my ideal day off, and it would be planned down to the minute. (4)

3. Complete the sentence: *When my mind wanders, it most often goes first to . . .*
    a. The people in my life (1)
    b. What I need to do that day (2)
    c. What my life might look like in the future (3)
    d. Strategy for how to get where I want to be in life (4)

4. How does it feel when you have to sit down to write knowing there's other stuff you need to get done that day?
    a. Fine (3)
    b. Not great, but tolerable (1)
    c. Completely untenable—I can't work until they're out of the way. (2)
    d. Irrelevant question—I don't start until I've already done them. (4)

5. What most accurately completes this sentence? *During the time between when I sit down and when I actually begin writing, I am usually . . .*
    a. Checking phone, email, news, social media (1)
    b. Daydreaming about what it will be like when I finish my project (3)
    c. Completing small tasks so I have them out of the way and can concentrate (2)
    d. Starting a sentence, reading it, deleting it, and repeat (4)

6. What do you most often end up doing instead of writing?
    a. Reading my journal (3)
    b. Chores (2)
    c. Email or other communication (1)
    d. Sitting there getting frustrated (4)

7. What would most help you focus?
    a. If an electromagnetic pulse wiped out the Internet (1)
    b. If I was like the main character of the film *Memento*, with no memory of the past and no concept of the future (3)
    c. If, every time I stopped typing (or writing), a rabid nun whapped my hands with a ruler (4)
    d. If I had a butler who would take care of my every need (2)

8. Which word do you think best describes you—if you had to pick just one?
   a. Efficient (2)
   b. Fun (1)
   c. Talented (4)
   d. Creative (3)

Tally up your score based on the numbers beside each answer. Your score will tell you which of these descriptions best applies to you.

- 8–15: You're a people person and love being connected. Flitting from screen to screen, you're always in touch in one way or another. One of the aspects you most dislike about writing is how it cuts you off from the world—you're not a fan of the isolation that comes with it. You crave interaction and have to make a real effort to "unplug" in order to focus. The Threshold Guardian you are most likely to struggle with is the Hydra.

- 16–23: There's no feeling you love more than crossing tasks off your To Do list. It's tough for you to set aside a big chunk of time to write when plenty of other obligations are tugging at you—and it's incredibly tempting to do what comes easily or quickly instead of writing, especially when you know it's possible you could spend hours at your computer with few tangible results to show. The Threshold Guardian you are most likely to struggle with is the Hydra.

- 24–31: An inveterate daydreamer, it's easy for you to get lost in your fantasies, whether they're memories of the past or your vision or worries about the future. You're capable of working hard, but you'd rather relax and let your mind wander than knuckle down. You have a tendency to get ten steps ahead of yourself—you're only a few chapters into your novel, and already you're planning where to hold the launch party when it gets published. The Threshold Guardian you are most likely to struggle with is the Rakshasa.

- 32: You seek perfection in all things, and especially from yourself. You have a highly attuned sense of what you consider good writing and what you don't, and the minute you see anything that's not your best work on the page, you pounce on it and tear it apart. As a result, you hate writing even a sentence that isn't excellent, so you often freeze up and find yourself sitting at the computer obstinately when you can't get into the zone where the work feels like it's flowing well. The Threshold Guardian you are most likely to struggle with is the Troll.

Now that you've pinpointed your most aggravating Threshold Guardian, let's explore what the Hydra, Rakshasa, and Troll are—and why they're so insidious to your process.

THE MANY-HEADED HYDRA

Trisha was under contract to write her second novel. But she was running a little behind. She had missed her delivery date by five years—and she still hadn't finished the manuscript.

She'd written eighty or so pages, but couldn't seem to get any further. Every time she tried to sit down to write, she felt pulled in a dozen different directions at once. There were always emails to respond to, chores that needed taking care of around the house, children to be driven to soccer practice and choir rehearsal. Not to mention all the projects she'd promised herself she'd tackle—like rebuilding her author website, maintaining her social media presence so she'd get invited to do more speaking engagements, and preparing for those events when she did them.

She set aside time to write—and she never used it for writing. Meanwhile, her book was getting later . . . and later . . . and later.

The Guardian keeping Trisha from getting into her writing zone was the Hydra.

The Hydra, a multiheaded snake creature from Greek mythology, is a perfect symbol for the diversions that can invade the writing process. There are always a million excuses not to write, and a million things to do instead. Chores, errands, tasks, social media, email and other communication, falling down an Internet rabbit hole—each one is a serpent's head, waving at us, tempting us to succumb. When you cut one distraction off—by turning off your phone, disconnecting from the Internet, or closing your door—it can feel as if two more grow in its place.

The diversions of the Hydra can also take the form of superstitions or limiting beliefs about the perfect conditions we "need" in order to write. "I can only write in the morning . . . at my favorite coffee shop . . . when I can get the table I like . . . if the barista smiles at me when I walk in the door." If you find yourself falling into such superstitions, at least you're in talented company. It's said that Truman Capote would never start or complete any piece of writing on a Friday, Alexandre Dumas would only write fiction on a certain shade of blue paper, and John Steinbeck insisted on having twelve sharpened pencils sitting on his desk at all times.

It's easy to blame the Hydra on technology and the way it splinters our attention, but centuries before phones and Internet made us so connected, writers still had to fight for focus. When Gustave Flaubert was working on *Madame Bovary*, he was caring for his aging mother, tutoring his five-year-old niece, running their household, and could only write after the rest of the family had gone to bed. Sylvia Plath juggled motherhood, housekeeping, and writing and struggled her entire brief life to find time and focus.

Most of us have busy, full, fragmented lives, and it's hard to simply forget about them and write as if nothing else in the world existed—at least before you cross the Threshold into flow.

THE MANIPULATING RAKSHASA

Cho had a different problem. After a short story he'd written won a prize, he'd decided to put together a collection and try to submit it to publishers. But he was having a hard time completing his second story.

Whenever his mind was idle—on his commute, at the gym, while making dinner—Cho would fantasize about what his life would be like when his short story collection had been published. He tried to picture what the cover would look like. He daydreamed about winning the National Book Award and fretted over whom to thank in his acceptance speech. When he actually sat down, though, he couldn't manage to get anything on the page.

The Guardian Cho was dealing with was a Rakshasa.

Human-eating monsters from Hindu mythology, these creatures—whose name means "Protect me!" in Sanskrit—possess giant fangs, scythe-like fingernails, and the power to create visions that seem so real, they completely fool the humans in the creatures' thrall.

It can be easy to fall into the trap of daydreaming, recalling memories from the past or fantasizing about the future. You may lose yourself in the sepia-hazy memories of the more inspired, more productive writing times of yore or you might be like Cho, dreaming of future success. Conversely, you may be worrying about what will happen if you *don't* finish your project, envisioning future failure. Or you could get stuck in the web of the *If only* wish list (*If only I had . . .* [more money/my own workspace/more time/a job/no job/a different job/true love/a cigarette] . . . then *I could write.*)

However they manifest themselves to you, these visions, like those fabricated by a Rakshasa, can be utterly stymieing.

THE TROLL WITH THE TERRIBLE MIRROR

I met Ophelia in a class I taught about getting over writer's block. Near tears, she described how frustrating it was to sit in front of her computer, day after day, trying to write. She wouldn't get further than a sentence or two before she'd delete it and start over. She insisted that whatever she'd written was awful. It was clear that her perfectionist streak sat squarely in the driver's seat when she was writing and refused to let her leave anything on the page that she felt was anything less than brilliant.

Her Threshold Guardian was a Troll.

This isn't the sort of troll you had as a kid, with mad-scientist hair, a beatific expression, and a jewel in its belly. This Troll comes from the Hans Christian Andersen tale *The Snow Queen*, in which he (the Troll) creates a magic mirror that reflects only the villainous, ugly aspects of whatever appears in it, magnifying the worst and hiding anything good. This is just the sort of perfectionism that can freeze you in your tracks, just as the heart of the little boy in *The Snow Queen* becomes frozen when a shard of the mirror gets into his eye. With the Troll's mirror obscuring your view of your writing, you can only see its flaws and you can't create.

WHY WON'T THEY LEAVE US ALONE?

All these Threshold Guardians have the ability to prevent you from diving fully into your writing. The next time you sit down to write, notice who pops up to block your passage to the magical world of focus. Is it the Hydra, waving its many heads, yanking your attention in countless directions? The Rakshasa, filling your mind with stories about your life? Or the Troll with his mirror, freezing your hands above the keys?

The first step is to identify who's holding you back. The second step is to find out why.

Threshold Guardians, like mosquitoes, can seem irritating, dangerous, and useless. But in fact, much like mosquitoes, they exist for a reason. Mosquitoes are bat food; Guardians, too, have a purpose. The key to managing Threshold Guardians lies in recognizing where they came from, what they're doing, and their inherent value.

EXERCISE: WHERE THE WILD THINGS COME FROM

If you've identified which Threshold Guardian presents the greatest obstacle to you, you can go straight to its section in the exercise. If they're all troubling you, do all three.

Hydra: Diversions

Go back to the Character Sheet exercise from chapter one. Using this version of you as a Hero, write a narrative description of yourself arriving at the Threshold and encountering the Hydra. Write the scene from your point of view. Be sure to go into detail about what the Hydra looks like, acts like, and how it distracts you.

Now write the same scene again, but from the Hydra's point of view. What's its motivation for trying to distract you? Why is it guiding you in so many directions away from your writing? Again, use details.

Looking at these two descriptions, consider these questions as jumping-off points for further introspection:

- How and why was this Hydra created?

- How is it trying to help you? What would be a better way for it to accomplish that?

- Why might a part of you feel that doing other tasks is somehow more beneficial to you than writing?

- What are you afraid might happen if you really allow yourself to focus and lose yourself in the work?

Write one more version of the scene. In this one, the image of the Mentor that you created in chapter four appears and reveals that she or he placed this Threshold Guardian here.

More questions to explore:

- What might your Mentor be trying to teach or show you about yourself with this Hydra?

- What is your Mentor challenging you to do in order to overcome this monster and get on with your journey?

Rakshasa: Fantasies

Go back to the Character Sheet exercise from chapter one. Using this version of you as a Hero, write a narrative description of yourself arriving at the Threshold and encountering the Rakshasa. Write the scene from your point of view. Be sure to go into detail about what the Rakshasa looks like, acts like, and the visions it creates.

Now write the same scene again, but from the Rakshasa's point of view. What's its motivation for weaving these illusions? What is it trying to show you? Again, use details.

Looking at these two descriptions, consider these questions as jumping-off points for further introspection:

- How and why was this Rakshasa created?

- How is it trying to help you? What would be a better way for it to accomplish that?

- What is the Rakshasa trying to tell you about yourself in these fantasies?

- What makes these fantasies feel like a safer place than getting into flow?

- What do the fantasies offer you that you aren't getting in your real life?

Write one more version of the scene. In this one, the image of the Mentor that you created in chapter four appears and reveals that she or he placed this Threshold Guardian here.

More thought questions to explore:

- What might your Mentor be trying to teach or show you about yourself with this Rakshasa?

- What is your Mentor challenging you to do to overcome this monster and get on with your journey?

Troll: Perfectionism

Go back to the Character Sheet exercise from chapter one. Using this version of you as a Hero, write a narrative description of yourself arriving at the Threshold and encountering the Troll with the mirror. Write the scene from your point of view. Be sure to go into detail about what the Troll looks like and what happens when he holds up his mirror.

Now write the same scene again, but from the Troll's point of view. What's his motivation for showing you yourself and your writing in the mirror? How does he think he's doing you a favor? Again, use details.

Looking at these two descriptions, consider these questions as jumping-off points for further introspection:

- How and why was this Troll created?

- How is he trying to help you? What would be a better way for him to accomplish that?

- What is the Troll afraid will happen if you write imperfectly?

- What makes writing nothing at all seem more beneficial than writing imperfectly?

- What will happen if you continue to write nothing?

Write one more version of the scene. In this one, the image of the Mentor that you created in chapter four appears and reveals that she or he placed this Threshold Guardian here.

More thought questions to explore:

- What might your Mentor be trying to teach or show you about yourself with this Troll and his mirror?

- What is your Mentor challenging you to do to overcome this monster and get on with your journey?

———————

Helpful Hindrances

When forced to confront the source of her Hydra, Tricia acknowledged that she was allowing herself to be diverted because she was avoiding a story problem in her novel. She thought if she kept pushing herself, she'd eventually figure it out on the page, but instead, she kept bouncing off her manuscript into other tasks that required less critical thinking.

Once she recognized this as the source of the distraction, she was able to focus on solving the story problem rather than trying to push herself through it. When she finally resolved it—by taking some time away from the manuscript, letting her thoughts marinate during some long walks, and talking it through with her editor—she found focusing somewhat easier, though it continued to be a challenge. Going forward, when she caught herself falling into those patterns of avoidance, remembering the motivation beneath them helped her curb them before she fell into another long rut.

Cho was drifting into fantasy so easily because he felt frustrated and bored with his life. Winning the contest had been exciting and had created an expectation that writing could be his ticket out of his current situation: stuck in a job he disliked without a strong sense of goals or purpose. Once he recognized this, though, he was able to admit that writing with intention was a lot harder than his first story had been, which had come to him in a burst of inspiration. He had to rethink his motivations and found that writing was still important to him, but he approached it very differently.

When Ophelia did a rigorous self-examination, she discovered the source of her perfectionism. Every time she sat down to write, she felt tremendous responsibility to be incredibly clear about her meaning. She worried that as an African American woman, writing about the particular subjects she tackled opened her up for potential criticism and misunderstanding. She hated the thought of her work being misinterpreted, because the themes she was addressing—and the criticism her work leveled at aspects of the African American community as she'd experienced it—were tremendously important to her.

Knowing this didn't magically relieve the pressure or take away the anxiety she felt. But the awareness of where her Threshold Guardian was coming from helped her coax herself forward and remind herself why she was writing to begin with.

These hindrances to writing can often come from a helpful impulse gone wrong or one that may have been more relevant at an earlier time in your life but has outlived its usefulness. The Hydra might be distracting you from inherent issues within the work that you don't want to address or from the fact that you may need to go deeper with it emotionally than you feel ready to. Those daydreams and fantasies of the Rakshasa can be a result of insecurities, about the work or about yourself. The Troll can come from the impulse to be your own worst critic so nobody else can hurt you or to spare you the supposed shame or embarrassment that would result from your work being exposed in its raw state. In all these cases, the monsters are trying to protect you from pain, stress, dealing with fears, and challenging yourself.

The trouble is, challenging yourself is exactly what's required for doing your best writing, completing a project, and undergoing the Hero's Journey of the writing process. In a weird Catch-22, in their efforts to prevent you from challenging yourself, these Threshold Guardians you've created are offering you a different challenge: to get past them and into your writing flow.

> *Challenging yourself is exactly what's required for doing your best writing, completing a project, and undergoing the Hero's Journey of the writing process.*

In myth, Hercules kills the Hydra by chopping off each snake-head and cauterizing the neck with his nephew's help so two more heads can't grow to replace it, until the creature is completely decapitated. Rakshasas are killed in various ways in different stories, usually by brute strength in a duel, often by a magical weapon blessed by a god or goddess, and sometimes while being distracted by monkeys. As for the Troll, the fragment of his mirror that plagues the boy in *The Snow Queen* is finally melted by the tears of the boy's best friend, the girl who saves him from his frozen state. But the Troll himself is never dispatched.

You'll notice that in all three of these examples, the Heroes didn't shake off these monsters all alone. If you're struggling to stay focused, try enlisting the help of an Ally. Particularly when Allies provide accountability, they often force you to shut out distractions and tune out fantasies, and there's nothing like sitting right across from another writer who's typing away to get your fingers hitting the keys, no matter what's coming out.

Taking a page from the ways Heroes in stories deal with their Threshold Guardians, let's try some of their approaches on yours.

EXERCISE: IGNORE, ABSORB, ACKNOWLEDGE–AND MOVE ON

In *The Writer's Journey*, screenwriting guru Christopher Vogler lists three ways that Heroes in stories typically dispense with Threshold Guardians. Try out all of them on different days when your particular monster is plaguing you to see how each one works for you. Keep in mind the strengths you identified in chapter one; how can you use those to your best advantage here?

METHOD 1: Ignore them. The threat they present is an illusion and a test of your mettle, so have faith in yourself and simply push past them.

How to practice it . . .

. . . **ON THE HYDRA:** Turn off your phone, get an Internet-blocking app for your computer, or skip the computer entirely and write longhand. Tell everyone you have set aside this time for writing and not to disturb you. If anyone intrudes, say you are working on deadline and will get back to them when you are done for the day. If you're more distracted by your To Do list than by being connected, find a space to work where you are removed from as many of your potential tasks as possible, ideally outside your home. Even within projects, you can find tasks to do, so only open the document that contains your draft and put your computer in a mode that blocks out the rest of your screen. Leave your To Do list at home.

. . . **ON THE RAKSHASA:** If you find your mind wandering into those fantasy realms, coax it back by thinking about just the next step of your project. (For example, writing the next scene or the next chapter.) Resist the urge to read books about the end goal (like how to get published or how to sell a screenplay) and focus your efforts on purely studying craft.

. . . **ON THE TROLL:** Don't begin each writing session by reading what you wrote last time; instead, just start. If you find yourself spending more than five minutes stuck on any one part of the piece, skip it, write yourself a note about what will eventually go there, and move on to a part that inspires you more. You can download a program that will start eating what you've written, word by word, if your fingers remain idle for a certain amount of time—nothing like a little panic to keep you moving!

METHOD 2: ABSORB THEM. Take them in or "become" them by slipping into their skin, seeing things from their perspective, trying to figure out their original purpose, and consuming what's useful about them, leaving the rest. (We did some of this in the previous exercise, so you can use that to inform your actions here.)

How to practice it:

. . . **ON THE HYDRA:** Focus on what the distractions may be allowing you to avoid. Begin your writing session without the expectation of "accomplishing" or finishing anything—forget about word count, page count, and specific achievement targets you might have been trying to hit. Make the goal of this session simply to discover why you're failing to find the same satisfaction from writing that you can get in a quick fix from crossing something smaller off your list. If something in the piece isn't working, don't be afraid to look at it honestly, knowing that you will ultimately find a solution. If you don't like feeling socially isolated, write with an Ally who won't enable you by chatting and will motivate you to get in there and get messy with whatever roadblock you're running into in the work.

. . . **ON THE RAKSHASA:** Ask yourself what you're getting from those daydreams that you're not finding in your conscious life. Does it have to do with the specific project you're writing, or is it broader, connected with your identity or the way you see yourself? Imagine what would happen if nobody ever saw your writing—would you still be motivated to do it? What can you extract from your daydreams that can turn them into a source of motivation rather than a source of distraction? Pull out that useful aspect and create a reminder of it that you post in your workspace.

. . . **ON THE TROLL:** Ask what exactly your expectations are of yourself, and whether they are realistic. When you catch yourself deleting your own words, jot down exactly what the Troll in your head is saying and read it out loud to see what it sounds like. Think about the Troll's mirror; what would a reverse version of that mirror be like, one that only showed the very best qualities in your writing, magnified, and excluded the flaws? What do you love most about your own work?

METHOD 3: ACKNOWLEDGE THEM. "Like tipping a doorman or paying a ticket-taker at a theatre," says Vogler, give them some credit and move along on your journey.

How to practice it:

. . . **ON THE HYDRA:** For those distracted by being connected, your love of people is a great gift, and you can extract tremendous value from it at other moments when you're not trying to write. Don't belittle your urge to be plugged in—acknowledge how much the people in your life mean to you and how much you appreciate them. Set aside a chunk of time, after you've accomplished your writing for the day, when you can do something social to blow off steam and celebrate meeting your goal. For those more commonly distracted by tasks, your productivity and zeal for getting things done are admirable and enviable, and serve you well. Take a moment to feel good about all the things you've already gotten done this week, rather than focusing on what you have yet to do. It can help to keep a To Do list that shows everything you've already crossed off. Put only one item on your To Do list for today: write. And promise yourself that, after you've crossed that off your list, anything else you get done is gravy.

. . . **ON THE RAKSHASA:** The ability to let your mind wander and ramble is actually essential to creativity, so you're fortunate that this comes naturally to you. You just have to know when and how to rein it in. Instead of fighting the fantasies when they appear, appreciate whatever they are showing you that is helpful and what you're learning from the emotions that arise from these fantasies. Put your powers of visualization to work for you—rather than picturing your life when the entire project is complete, create a mental vision of how you will accomplish the next step of it. People who envision *how* to achieve their goals are much more likely to meet those goals.

. . . **ON THE TROLL:** Known for your good taste, you have a keen mind, a discerning eye, and a strong bullshit detector. You are probably a terrific editor of your friends' writing. Acknowledge your talent for critique and assessment, which will serve you very well when you reach the revision part of the process. Put that gift on a shelf to save for that later stage, and give your other gift—your talent for writing—room to breathe without being constricted by the inner editor. Promise yourself that nobody but you will see this draft, and you'll have the opportunity to make it better later. Think about how much you'll enjoy getting to refine it once you have enough on the page to work with.

———————————

The Monsters in Your Life

Chances are if these monsters are hampering your writing process, they may be affecting other areas of your life, too.

Herculean battlers of the Hydra, what are you missing out on while you're glued to your phone or your To Do list? How are social media, email, and busy-person tasks distracting you from aspects of your life? If you feel constantly consumed by the Hydra that tugs you in a million tiny directions, it may be worth taking a brief sabbatical from a few of your most pervasive snake-heads and allowing yourself more time and mental space to simply think your thoughts.

If you've noticed you are prone to fragmented focus, observe whether this also makes you vulnerable to chronic nagging anxiety. Says Daniel Goleman, "The power to disengage our attention from one thing and move it to another is essential for well-being"—not just for writing.

How can you create more boundaries in your life around the challengers to your focus? One coaching client told me she wanted to be productive in the morning but often got derailed because each day, as soon as she woke up, she picked up her phone from her bedside table and scrolled through the headlines, her social media feeds, and email to see what she'd missed while asleep. She was shocked and delighted by my suggestion that she not keep her phone in her bedroom. Boundaries are built one small choice at a time, and a simple change can make a big difference.

> *How can you create more boundaries in your life around the challengers to your focus?*

If you frequently catch yourself tuning out the present moment in favor of memories, worries, or fantasies, ask yourself what you're escaping from in the here and now. What do you find difficult about being present? What makes the Rakshasa's visions more appealing than your reality? Unless you're an adherent of string theory, all that really exists is the present; everything else is merely a figment in our minds. What moments might be passing you by as you fantasize about an alternate life? What about your reality are you avoiding looking at or experiencing head-on?

Even when it is painful, the present moment is precious—especially for writers, because it's constantly yielding fodder for the page. If you fully experience it, rather than seeking escape from it, you're more likely to confront the unpleasant aspects of it and ask what you have the power to change. Life puts us in many situations that we have no control over, but that's why it's so important to identify what we *can* affect.

Boundaries are built one small choice at a time, and a simple change can make a big difference.

The next time you catch yourself drifting into these fantasies, practice mindfulness: simply notice that your mind is taking you elsewhere, without judging yourself for it. Watch your thoughts with curiosity and notice whether there are certain times or situations when your mind instinctively dives for that escape hatch. Bringing attention to this predilection each time it happens can be the first step toward more directly and openly experiencing your own life.

If you are a perfectionist about your writing, there's a good chance you apply that same critical gaze to other parts of your life. What else are you holding the Troll's mirror up to? How are you turning that judgmental gaze on yourself to see only the flaws—and what qualities might that perspective be forcing you to overlook?

We all have moments when we need to push ourselves harder, or can benefit from a healthy dose of sobering perspective to remind us we're not the only special snowflakes in the world. But many people who've taken this to heart have a tendency to overcorrect. I've seen numerous writers place unrealistic standards and expectations on themselves that they'd never dream of imposing on another person. When they look at their progress with their writing, their professional successes, their relationships, their appearances, the time and attention they devote to eating healthfully and exercising, they only see flaws and failures.

There's nothing wrong with having high standards as long as they serve you, but when they become an excuse for inaction or a justification for self-cruelty, they lose their value. In all my years as a coach, I've not yet seen someone who got much of worth out of beating herself up or putting himself down.

A tendency to see yourself through the Troll's mirror isn't something you can just snap out of, but noticing you're doing it is often the first step toward softening that view.

Keep in mind, there's nothing inherently wrong with enjoying staying plugged in, pursuing productivity, having a mind that wanders, or being discerning. These traits have equal potential for hindering you or for being gifts that serve you well in life. It's all in how you use them.

Small Steps Across the Threshold

During the course of our work together, Gary continued to struggle with distraction. Every day he faced the Hydra of leading a very plugged-in life and being addicted to the feeling of accomplishment that came with any size of job completed. The Rakshasa often sent him into daydreams about life after publishing his book even though he still hadn't written more than a chapter. The Troll made him quick to abandon what he was writing if it wasn't brilliant within the first few minutes of his sitting down.

By the conclusion of coaching, all this was still true. But Gary had developed coping tools to help himself when he fell into his familiar patterns. He'd found a partner in accountability, an Ally who helped him set deadlines and made the writing experience feel more social, serving his desire for connection and giving him more manageable benchmarks to feed that need for accomplishment. He'd let go of his limiting beliefs about where and when he could be creative, and started using his daily time on the train to freewrite, warming up his writing muscles. The more he got down on the page, the more he wanted to keep going—even if it wasn't perfect.

The flip side of getting distracted, sidetracked, and locked up is that, once you break through the noise and begin writing in earnest, being in that flow feels better than ever. The satisfaction of overcoming these obstacles allows you to derive even deeper satisfaction from your work than if the writing had come effortlessly. Each time you get the upper hand against these neurotic tendencies, you walk away from the experience empowered, knowing you're capable of overcoming them.

The satisfaction of overcoming these obstacles allows you to derive even deeper satisfaction from your work than if the writing had come effortlessly.

So the next time you find yourself procrastinating, daydreaming, or being a perfectionist, use the methods you've developed here. Remind yourself that you've beat that Guardian before and you will beat it again. And remember that perfection, like the monsters we've met in this chapter, is only a myth.

EXERCISE: MID-BOOK CHECK-IN

Now that you've crossed the Threshold and are well into your adventure, it's a good time to look at your progress and how you're feeling about it. Answer the self-assessment questions about each exercise or chapter.

Return to the Character Sheet exercise in chapter one.

1. PROJECT VISION: Has the vision for your project changed since you stated it at the beginning of our process?

     If you have any alterations to this vision statement—new reasons why this piece is important to you or a different way you are thinking about the project now that you're further into it—write your revised statement.

2. SKILLS: Rate yourself on these various skills again, now that we've put some of them to work.

   - Inspiration
   - Connection
   - Intuition
   - Focus
   - Resilience
   - Patience
   - Courage
   - Flexibility
   - Confidence

     Notice whether you got the same ratings or if any numbers changed, and if so, which and how much.

     If your scores changed, did your Greatest Strength and Greatest Vulnerability change? If so, write the new ones down.

3. GREATEST VULNERABILITY: Identify one to three moments since you began this process when you've struggled with the vulnerability you identified in the Character Sheet exercise.

For each one, write what you did to address it and say whether or not you ultimately found this effective.

Reflect on what have you discovered about it—and about yourself—through finding ways to work with it, and jot down a few sentences.

4. MAP: Where are you on the route you outlined toward your goal in chapter one?

    Note how far you have come based on whatever system you are using to measure your progress. For example, if each square on the path represents an amount of time, a word count, or a page count, add up how much you've accumulated since you began. You may have already been keeping a running count.

    Are you going at the pace you predicted, or more slowly or quickly?

    Have you taken any surprising detours? Describe the most unexpected in a sentence.

5. Looking at all the chapters you've worked through so far, which exercise(s) have resonated/helped the most? List your favorite(s).

6. Which did you find the least helpful or did you have the hardest time with? List it/them.

7. Name one challenge you wish a future exercise would help you address.

As you read over your answers, notice whether anything surprises you, frustrates you, or makes you especially happy or proud.

Hang on to all the information you've gleaned from the exercise. We'll use it again later.

———————————————

CHAPTER SIX

the shapeshifter

change your point of view

After crossing the Threshold, the Hero has finally gained entrance to the magical world. Known in myth as the "Ordeal" or the "Road of Trials," this part of the journey takes the Hero through foreign landscapes and into encounters with characters who can be helpful or harmful. Any Hero who enters this period of the journey with specific expectations or plans is likely to have them thwarted.

As a writer, you may have plotted out a map to your goal, assembled everything you need to help you, and gotten started—even found methods for pushing past distraction. Now you have to use the systems or structures you've created to keep writing, day . . . after day . . . after day. The writer's "Road of Trials" is the path to project completion. One of the greatest rewards you can glean from this "Ordeal" is a writing practice that keeps you working, not just when you get inspired or feel in the mood, but on a regular basis, as a normal part of your life.

This is where I spend the bulk of my time with the writers I coach: walking

The more tools you have at your disposal, the better equipped you'll be to address whatever the next bump in the road might be.

down the Road of Trials together, observing what comes up, keeping an eye out for pitfalls, and focusing on moving forward. Whatever challenge a writer is dealing with today can be totally different from the ones that come up tomorrow, next week, or two months from now. The more tools you have at your disposal, the better equipped you'll be to address the next bump in the road. And the archetypes you meet on the Road of Trials can provide you with some of those tools.

The Shapeshifter

Heroes in stories often encounter characters whose motives are murky, or whose morals are unclear. When Heroes decide to take a risk and trust these strangers, they have no idea what they're in for. A seemingly guileless individual who appears to be an Ally may deliver the Hero directly into the hands of enemies, or a shady person who seems worthy of suspicion could wind up saving the Hero's life. Such characters are changeable, unpredictable, and often a little bit magical. They're **Shapeshifters**.

Shapeshifters are characters that change their form—some literally, like a witch or werewolf, some figuratively. Anyone who isn't what he or she appeared to be at first blush, or who has hidden facets, can be considered a Shapeshifter. If that sounds like a vague definition, that's part of the Shapeshifter's inherent intangibility—the difficulty of identifying them is often what allows them to gain the upper hand over Heroes.

Anyone who isn't what he or she appeared to be at first blush, or who has hidden facets, can be considered a Shapeshifter.

The Shapeshifter archetype represents the changeability of human nature, and we are a decidedly changeable group. We all have the shapeshifting impulse—that temptation most of us have felt to try out a different identity when traveling, moving to a new place, or starting a job. Even something as simple as a different haircut or a new article of clothing can give us a sense of feeling like someone a little unfamiliar. This is why many people love (and some loathe) Halloween—it's an opportunity to transform yourself into a stranger and walk for a day in an alien skin.

Of course, the greatest locus of shapeshifting today is the Internet, which allows people to live whole lives hidden behind personas of their own creation. From gaming avatars to forum screen names to the curated version of ourselves we feed out on social media, we are all Shapeshifters in the vast online landscape with endless potential for mutating identities.

Writers are natural Shapeshifters. Putting ourselves into the shoes of others and imagining what life would look like through their eyes is a major element of writing. For craft, shapeshifting is essential, and is a muscle you've likely already been toning for years. We're going to take that ability and apply to your process.

> *Writers are natural Shapeshifters.*

In this chapter, we'll look at how to shapeshift into your complete opposite, into a cast of characters who can give you multiple perspectives and skills, and into a writer-observer even when you're far away from the writing room.

Going Undercover

Cari Lynn worked on the floor of the Chicago Mercantile Exchange, the busiest futures market in the world. Few women were employed in the pits of the "Merc," and the female traders she admired clawed their way through each day of buying and selling surrounded by hundreds of cutthroat traders, mostly male and mostly determined to make their female counterparts miserable. It was, she told me, "vicious, violent, and incredibly high stakes."

This was in 2000, and the money to be made in trading was obscene. As a result, the competition was murderous; only those tough enough to hack their way through the gauntlet of harassment, bullying, and fighting that came with the job reaped the financial rewards.

But Cari was in it for the story.

Cari had no background in finance. She was a journalist based in Chicago. After becoming fascinated by the stories her neighbor told her about being a woman in the boys' club of futures trading, Cari knew she had to write a book on the subject. And the best way to do that, she found, was by immersing herself in this world that was unlike anything she'd known or experienced before.

Every morning as soon as she woke up, she turned on CNBC. She'd never bought the *Wall Street Journal* in her life; now it was daily required reading. She spent her days working at the Merc and her nights hanging out with other traders at the private clubs they frequented—she got some of her best material when her subjects were loosened up with liquor and away from the trading floor.

To write her book, Cari had changed her form. She was way beyond being a mere observer in this world; she'd become a citizen of it.

But Cari never lost sight of the real reason she was there, and after two years of total immersion, she knew it was time to step away from living the lifestyle and start focusing on writing the story of her experiences and those of the other women she'd met. The result, her book *Leg the Spread: Adventures Inside the Trillion-Dollar Boys' Club of Commodities Trading*, came out in 2004.

Cari's is an extreme example, but many of us have experienced a version of what she went through. Have you ever held a job at which nobody knew you were a writer? Do you have to shift back and forth between a major role you play in your life—parent, partner, professional, leader—and your more private role as a writer? Are there people in your life with whom you don't share the fact that you write? Have you ever drawn material for your writing from experiences you've had out in the world?

If you answered "yes" to any of these questions, you have already employed the Shapeshifter archetype in your life.

But the Shapeshifter is more than simply a tool to apply to your identity. It can become an integral part of your writing process.

Reading Like a Stranger

Wouldn't it be nice if you could read your work with the eyes of a stranger? Many writers try to simulate this experience to get a fresh perspective while working. Author George Saunders told me he comes to his desk each day with only one rule: he must read the draft with "first-reader mind," as if he's never seen a word of the story before. Comedy writer Negin Farsad prints out each draft of her screenplays and reads the text aloud in the voice of a child. Neil Gaiman advises budding writers, "Once it's done . . . put it away until you can read it with new eyes . . . When you're ready, pick it up and read it, as if you've never read it before."

It's not just your work that can benefit from fresh eyes. Seeing your entire process through the eyes of a stranger can give you insight into what you're doing that's not working well for you and how to tweak your methods to better serve your needs. Many writers come to me seeking an objective perspective on how they're working and help making beneficial changes. Sometimes, you're just too close to your own process, too deeply entrenched in it, to be able to see what might be obvious to an observer.

In this exercise, you'll shapeshift into that observer.

EXERCISE: CREATING YOUR OPPOSITE

Go back to the profile of yourself that you created in the Character Sheet exercise in chapter one and updated in the Mid-Book Check-In.

Based on this profile, create a character that is your opposite in every way and make a new Character Sheet for this person with the template that follows. Use your imagination to come up with someone who looks, behaves, and experiences the world totally differently from you. There are many ways to interpret the idea of opposition—physical, psychological, emotional, intellectual, and so on—and I encourage you to explore them all. This individual might not even be human or live in our world. Or the character may simply be a person whose life couldn't be more different than yours.

Create an image of your Opposite.

NAME: Choose a name for your Opposite.

HISTORY AND DESCRIPTION: Give a brief bio and description of your Opposite.

SKILLS: Rate your Opposite with the inverse of your own scores in each category.

- Inspiration
- Connection
- Intuition
- Focus
- Resilience
- Patience
- Courage
- Flexibility
- Confidence

Based on the scores in SKILLS, identify your Opposite's Greatest Strength and Greatest Vulnerability.

GEAR: What does this individual always carry when leaving home? For example, if you're a technophobe, your Opposite might have all the latest gadgets. If you're a pack rat, your Opposite might be a sleek minimalist. List what your Opposite can't live without.

TREASURE: What is your Opposite's special gift?

Now that you've created your Opposite, you have a tool through which you can filter any question that comes up during your writing process.

We'll use one as an example to get you started.

In the Mid-Book Check-In you identified one challenge you wished a future exercise would help you address. Write that challenge down again.

This is probably an issue you have been struggling with over time and have already tried addressing in the ways that came most naturally to you. But a completely different person would address it in a completely different way.

Channel your Opposite and write three things that individual would do or advise you to do about this issue.

Borrowing the perspective of your Opposite can yield insights that might not feel organic to you, but may end up being surprisingly helpful in getting you where you need to go.

Using Your Opposite

Creating a lens through which to see differently has applications far beyond your writing process. It can give you a new way to observe your life, whether you're at a crossroads, making a major decision, or simply trying to zoom out and gain perspective.

In his book *Redirect*, psychology professor Timothy D. Wilson cites several studies that have proven the value of examining our lives, particularly traumatic events in the past, from the point of view of "a neutral observer," which he says allows us to focus on "*why* you feel the way you do, rather than on the feelings themselves." In the studies, those who used this perspective on their lives were able to gain insight and move forward from the events they were reflecting on more quickly and lastingly than those who didn't.

You might use your Opposite to find this objectivity for situations in your life. Seeing your Opposite's take on any given decision or scenario in sharp relief with your own view might clarify feelings that may be murky for you. Sometimes, it takes an opposing viewpoint for us to identify exactly what we think or feel.

Luisa had been working for the same big company for several years while she wrote on the side. When she saw an opening at a startup, she figured it wouldn't hurt to apply, but after making it through several rounds of interviews and being offered the position, she wasn't sure what to do.

Her old job and this new position had comparable salaries and titles, and they both came with pros and cons. The new job would afford her more responsibility, which was exciting, but would also be more demanding on her schedule, taking time away from her writing, which was what she ultimately wanted to pursue. Her old job had grown somewhat stale, which was why she was seeking a new challenge, but felt more stable than working at a startup that still seemed to be figuring out its strategy. And the new job would involve a move, to a place she loved, but that would impact Luisa's relationship with her girlfriend, who wasn't in a position to easily relocate.

When Luisa tried to picture herself in the new role, she wasn't sure how she felt. So she tried looking at the situation from the point of view of her Opposite instead.

Luisa's Opposite was thrill-seeking, unconcerned about the relationship, and didn't prioritize writing. Focused on the rush of winning and the buzz of a new challenge, her Opposite was drawn to the possibilities in the new position—and instantly showed Luisa what kind of person she *didn't* want to be: one who takes the first opportunity that comes along, regardless of the impact it would have on the other facets of her life.

If her Opposite wanted the job, Luisa realized, she didn't. What she *did* want was to keep looking for something that might be a better fit, that wouldn't compromise her relationship and would give her what she was missing in her current role; and in the meantime, to focus more on her writing.

Creating a clear picture of who we aren't is a powerful way to remind us exactly who we are.

Seeing the situation through her Opposite's eyes showed her more clearly who she was, and helped her clarify who she wanted to become. Creating a clear picture of who we aren't is a powerful way to remind us exactly who we are.

Managing the Circus

Helen was stuck. A year earlier, she'd stepped off the corporate ladder to spend more time with her preschool-aged daughter and focus on her real passion: writing novels for ten- to twelve-year-olds. After burning out in the business world, she had felt completely ready to center her life around the things that mattered most to her: writing and family.

So why, she wondered, was she now feeling as stressed as she had in her corporate life?

She was struggling to concentrate. Every time she sat down and opened her manuscript, she ran right into a Threshold Guardian of perfectionism that froze her on the page. *You're no good at this,* the Troll whispered in her ear. She tried to ignore this voice, but her progress was slow, and she couldn't seem to shake the creeping sense that the Troll's nasty words were true. Going through this day after day became an anxiety-ridden slog.

She also felt an unusual lack of motivation. In her past career, Helen had been a go-getter who arrived early, stayed late, and was always overprepared for every meeting and presentation. But now, sitting alone in her home office with only the Troll for company, she was laboring to find that drive.

The more Helen talked to me about the Threshold Guardian that was bothering her, the more she began to realize that the Troll's voice wasn't the only one she could hear while she was working. As she explored the other characters that populated her psychic landscape, she began to envision a way to shapeshift into an array of roles that could help her get motivated and get writing. She just needed to define those voices more clearly and figure out how to make them useful—to turn what felt like neuroses into tools for her process.

For a decade, Helen had worked in a corporate high-rise surrounded by colleagues. So now, she built a personal mythology out of archetypes from the world that resonated with her, the world in which she'd been incredibly productive and gotten plaudits for her accomplishments: the office.

When she needed to inspire herself, she imagined she was a tough boss, giving a motivational speech to spur her employees on. When she needed to refine small details in her manuscript, she imagined she was a can-do assistant, attending to the little nuances to make sure everything was running smoothly with a smile on her face. When she needed to cast a calculating eye on her novel to make certain all the chapters were the same length and that the pacing was consistent, she imagined herself as the finance director, counting the beans and keeping the numbers in check.

By shapeshifting into these familiar roles whenever she needed them, she turned her unfamiliar new role—writer—into one that felt more comfortable. Identifying her own mythology and using its archetypes to create these roles for herself kept her from fixating on any one internal voice and helped her stay as motivated as she'd felt when all these characters were actually sitting in cubicles around her.

"When you say 'I'm an artist,'" George Saunders told me, "What that really means is that you have all these different manifestations of you, who work for you, and your job is to manage the circus." Saunders likened his own inner mythology to a construction crew—a group of people with a variety of skills, each doing different kinds of work, suited to the need at hand. It's his job, he said, to observe what skill, or worker, is needed for each situation.

"It's almost like a meditative experience to say, 'this person, me, actually isn't any one solid thing.' On any working day, these different personalities fluctuate on and off, and I can summon them, and I can tell them to back away at the end."

This book focuses on turning a particular mythology of archetypes into tools to address different needs in your process: the Hero's Journey. But you may find there's another mythology, one based more on your own history, life experiences, favorites, passions, and goals, that resonates with you even more.

EXERCISE: CREATING A PERSONAL MYTHOLOGY

Think about a social environment in which you feel comfortable or that feels familiar or resonant to you. It might be a place where you've accomplished things you're proud of; it could be somewhere you feel safe; or maybe it's where you feel most motivated. Comb through your past experiences and your fantasy life to choose a setting that best fits your needs. Some examples: school, workplace, family unit, athletic team, religious or spiritual community.

Write down the setting you've chosen.

Make a list of all the roles that exist in this setting. Don't think yet about which ones you'll use or how to use them—just get down everything you can think of. (For example, if you chose "school," some roles might include *teacher, class clown, valedictorian, principal, guidance counselor . . .*) These are the archetypes of your mythology.

Now put this list side by side with your self-assessment from the Mid-Book Check-In. Take note of each SKILL for which you rated yourself as less than a 5, especially your Greatest Vulnerability. Looking at your list here, ask yourself, *What archetype could I shapeshift into to best help me with each of these skills?*

Think about the challenge you used your Opposite to address in the previous exercise. How could shapeshifting into one of these roles help you tackle that issue in a new way? What archetype that you've listed here could be most helpful with your Threshold Guardians?

Based on these prompts, identify three to five archetypes that seem the most useful to you. For each one, write:

- A brief (two- to five-sentence) description of the archetype—physical appearance, personality, common behavior.

- A personal motto, written in the archetype's voice.

- A note to yourself about what situations this archetype might be most useful for.

If you want to flesh out your personal mythology more in ways I haven't listed here, I encourage you to do so. Either way, keep this roster of tools handy.

Turning Your Camera On

We've seen how the Shapeshifter can be a tool while at your desk. But it can also give you a lens for experiencing the world in a different way—one that can bring about a better integration of the writing and non-writing sides of your life.

Michael R. Jackson had worked at some pretty terrible jobs, but ushering had to be one of the worst. After leaving Detroit to study playwriting and musical theater writing in New York, Michael had spent the better part of a decade supporting himself with temp gigs and menial office jobs. But the nine-to-five workweek left him little time and energy at the end of the day to write. So Michael became an usher at Broadway's New Amsterdam Theatre, which housed the perennially popular show *The Lion King*.

Six days a week, at six evening shows and three matinees, Michael and his colleagues ran crowd control for 1,700 waddling tourists, screaming children, and wealthy grande dames. He saw a child run up the aisle, vomiting the entire length of the orchestra section. He saw an audience member leap onto the stage and scramble across it to find his seat on the other side mere seconds before the curtain went up. He saw the inebriated get escorted from the theater on a regular basis. When he operated the elevator to carry patrons up to the mezzanine and balcony, they would often, he told me, "fart and smile about it."

Night after night, as the subway carried him away from Times Square, he thought about quitting. But he needed the paycheck, and the gig gave him time to write in the mornings.

One particularly hellish Sunday afternoon, he and the other ushers had just started letting ticket-holders into the theater to sit down for the matinee performance. An elderly white woman had bypassed the staff in her charge to the mezzanine, but was now struggling to locate her seat. She held up her hand, waving her arm like she was flagging down a cab, and sang out at Michael, "Usher! Usher!"

That was when, as Michael told me, "my video camera went on." As a young black man, the experience of having an old white woman identify him by his job description and hail him like a taxi awoke something deep inside.

He'd already been working on a musical theater piece about a young gay black man in New York. It was a story about identity and family, but so far, it lacked cohesion, a framing device to tie it together. In that moment, Michael found his framing device: his protagonist would be an usher, just like him, and the entire show would take place against the backdrop of a Broadway theater.

The added component of *The Lion King* also fit perfectly with the themes Michael was exploring, and not just because the story of *The Lion King* also dealt with identity and family. Every day, he witnessed a huge arena full of largely white patrons watching black performers fetishize a fantasy of Africa for their entertainment, at $200 a ticket. To this spectacle, with all its layers of cultural context, Michael had had, in his words, "a front row seat from the back of the house every night for five years." He just hadn't realized what he was experiencing was all material for his art.

What had been a miserable job became a daily opportunity to do research and get inspired. Before, he'd tried to tune out the irritating theatergoers; now he observed them closely. The mundane tasks that used to bore him became fodder for his piece. Sitting in the lobby, stuffing programs with flyers for the next show, Michael often had so many ideas he had to jot them down on leftover programs.

Once he stopped experiencing his job as an usher and started experiencing it as a writer, both his work and his writing benefited. His job became imbued with purpose, and his writing took him deeper than he'd ever been able to go with a musical before. All it took was shapeshifting from one role to another—seeing himself not as an usher but as a writer.

Now, Michael says, "My video camera is always on."

Shapeshifting Away from Victimhood

When we see the world through a different lens—whether through our Opposite's eyes, as the foreperson of a cast of skilled workers we can deploy at will, or as a writer who can find inspiration anywhere—we take on the Shapeshifter's ability to change. But the Shapeshifter also reminds us of the danger of rigidity and complacency.

Shapeshifters in myth often appear just when Heroes seem to believe they've figured out the rules of the magical world. A Shapeshifter character will present the Hero with a deceptive appearance, then change form, leaving the Hero questioning reality. The Shapeshifter has reminded the Hero that circumstances can change in a second, and that the Hero needs to be prepared to change, too.

How often has this happened in your life? You approach a person or a situation believing you have a good handle on it, and then something alters and suddenly everything you believed turns out to have been wrong. You walk away shaken, less trusting of others and of your own ability to assess what's in front of you. And next time, you act differently.

When we step into the role of Shapeshifter, we are stepping into a role of power. We deepen our ability to become the source of change, rather than the victim of it. Like chameleons, when the world around us alters its form, we adapt.

Sharon Steel had dreamed of being a journalist since her first internship with a tiny local paper in college, and had spent seven years inching her way up the ladder, from Long Island to Boston to New York City, until she'd gotten a job at a New York City alternative weekly, *L Magazine*. It was her first full-time gig in New York, and she was proud of getting her foot in the door of the big city's competitive journalism scene.

It was the summer of 2008.

By the end of the year, it had become a nightmarish time to be in print journalism. With the economy tanking, readers were disappearing, and the Internet was devouring everything. Less than a month into 2009, Sharon was laid off.

She left the office with her belongings in plastic bags and called her best friend from the coffee shop around the corner in tears. Humiliated and ashamed of her failure, she was afraid she'd never find work again.

"Yes, you can," her friend told her firmly. "You can and you will."

As she made her way home, Sharon thought about the choice before her. She could let getting laid off define her. Or she could redefine herself.

That night, Sharon composed an email unlike any she'd ever written before. The subject line was "The Recession Takes Another Victim," but the tone conveyed anything but victimhood. In the email, she morphed from tearful to tough, wrapping a request for help finding work in the gift-wrap of witty jokes and clever commentary.

Before she could change her mind, she sent it to everyone she could think of who might be able to help—friends, acquaintances in the media, professional contacts.

Sharon was overwhelmed by the warmth and breadth of the response. People she hadn't heard from in ages wrote back generous replies expressing sympathy and support. The outpouring of love dried her tears and made her feel like she wasn't alone.

Over the next few weeks, work flowed in. Sharon's supportive network, and the confidence boost it gave her, helped her land pieces at publications she'd never dared pitch to before. Some of those pieces ultimately led to a full-time job at *Time Out New York*.

Sharon wrote her way out of unemployment. When she changed her shape, from one of "Victim" to Hero, she discovered how much was possible.

Shapeshifters don't truly become something else; they just show us a part of themselves we couldn't see before. When the circumstances on your own Road of Trials suddenly shift, whether they present you with a creative challenge or one that threatens your livelihood, remember the infinite possibility that lies within you. You can be your Opposite, the staff of an office, a construction crew, or a whole circus. And no matter what your job is, how you do your work, whom you do it for, or how other people perceive you, you are a writer.

Your capacity for change is limited only by your boundless imagination.

> *Shapeshifters don't truly become something else; they just show us a part of themselves we couldn't see before.*

CHAPTER SEVEN

the trickster

play, break your own rules, and remember to have fun

It was the early nineties, and George Saunders had hit rock bottom as a writer. He'd just graduated from an MFA program and was full of ideas about what a writer was supposed to be based on his literary role models Ernest Hemingway and Raymond Carver.

But George wasn't spending his days hunting big game or bolting whiskey. He was helping support his wife and their brand-new baby by working as a tech writer at a pharmaceutical company in an Albany office park where he was, he told me, "just the guy with a ponytail at a photocopier."

In his writing itself, he was also aiming to mirror Hemingway and Carver and failing. He'd just completed a three-hundred-page novel that seemed to him like a big turd sitting on his desk. He tried to mine the world around him for inspiration, to find pathos and poetry in the office park. But combining that setting with his imitation of his heroes' literary style yielded embarrassing results.

One day at work, he got stuck on a long, dull conference call. After sitting there for over an hour, he started writing dirty rhyming poems on his legal pad, just to stem the tedium. He augmented his scribbling with little funny drawings in the margins of the page as the call dragged on.

His doggerel and doodles entertained him so much he brought them home. When he showed them to his wife, also a writer, she told him it was the best writing he'd done in the past four years.

George had been working so hard he'd forgotten what came most naturally to him: making himself, and others, laugh. His friends and colleagues considered him a funny guy, and entertaining people felt easy. But he hadn't believed that his ability to make everyone around the water cooler crack up could ever benefit his writing. That behavior didn't fit with his notion of a literary writer.

When George acknowledged that his wife was right—that the version of him on the legal pad was more authentic and more interesting than all three hundred pages of his best Hemingway impression—he had to redefine his idea of what it meant to be a "literary" writer. He had to stop slogging and start entertaining himself.

Today, George Saunders is known for his wry short stories that pull the veil off and skewer institutions of American society with dark humor. He has received some of the highest honors in literature including the Story Prize, the PEN/Malamud Award, and the World Fantasy Award, all for being funny and being himself.

Tricksters ground Heroes, foster connection between people by provoking laughter, and highlight the foibles of society.

When he finally acknowledged the **Trickster** in him, his writing came alive.

Practical Jokers

When a Hero meets a character who is clever and wily, who has a wicked sense of humor and a penchant for mischief, who delights in riddles, puns, or pranks, and who often uses this antic nature to reveal a deeper truth, the Trickster has arrived—and the journey will never be the same.

The Trickster archetype provides comic relief in myth and in life. Tricksters ground Heroes, foster connection between people by provoking laughter, and highlight the foibles of society. Like Shapeshifters, they can be difficult to trust—and sometimes shouldn't be trusted—but can also prove to be staunch Allies who help Heroes in addition to making the stories they inhabit a whole lot more fun.

Outside of stories, Tricksters play an important role in the cultural conversation. Whether they're comedians like Amy Schumer and Key & Peele, artists like Andy Warhol and Banksy, or professional prankster groups like Improv Everywhere and The Masked Avengers, Tricksters highlight hypocrisies by tackling topics most people consider sacrosanct, subverting our expectations, and making us laugh and think.

The Trickster appears in each of us in different ways. Some people love playing pranks; others have mastered the one-liner; some reveal their inner Trickster via the Internet, while for others, the gag is all in the delivery. Though the Trickster emerges in moments of humor, this archetype is about more than just being funny—the Trickster points out that life is more surreal than we tend to acknowledge, that the emperor has no clothes.

Kurt Vonnegut once said, "If you make people laugh or cry about little black marks on sheets of white paper, what is that but a practical joke?" All writing is the work of the Trickster, and all writers have a spark of the Trickster within. The trouble is, we often forget about this side of ourselves at the moment when we need it most.

Taking anything too seriously is a surefire way to leach the pleasure out of it. You've been working hard for six chapters—so, stop. Take a break. Play. Laugh. Enjoy yourself. And discover that when you're at your most relaxed and silly, doing nothing that feels like "work," the Trickster may trick you into the greatest insights of your process so far.

All writing is the work of the Trickster, and all writers have a spark of the Trickster within.

Excising "Should"

In myth, Trickster characters often puncture Heroes' egos and force them to be more honest with themselves about their limitations. George Saunders was struggling because he had an inflated sense of what a writer was supposed to be. Once he let go of that, he was free to create the stories that felt most organic to him.

We often have such ideas about what kind of writing we "should" be doing, based on the families we grew up in, the educational environments we experienced, and the social pressures of our current lives. We internalize the expectations of others, and we create expectations for ourselves, but they don't always help us become better writers—and they often hinder us from writing what comes most naturally to us.

If you're feeling a bit like George was, unfurrow your brow and let this next exercise give you a break from your stress.

EXERCISE: AUDIENCE OF ONE

Forget what you "should" be writing. For the purposes of this exercise, we're going to put your project on hold. You can come back to it later.

Kurt Vonnegut said: "Every successful creative person creates with an audience of one in mind. That's the secret of artistic unity. Anybody can achieve it, if he or she will make something with only one person in mind. I didn't realize that [my sister] was the person I wrote for until after she died."

Choose a person from your life to be your audience of one for this exercise. Pick someone you know loves you, who doesn't judge you too harshly, whose expectations do not give you anxiety—someone whom it would give you great pleasure to entertain in whatever way that person most responds to.

Does this person love to laugh? To solve puzzles? To be inspired? Think about what kind of movies and television this person watches, the books this person reads, the music this person listens to, the activities this person enjoys doing. You could even, if you like, quiz the person about what he or she would find most entertaining and enjoyable in a written work.

You are going to create a piece of writing made expressly for this person. Answer the following questions about the piece you'll write, based on what you think your chosen person would take most delight in.

What form will it be? (A poem, story, song, joke, verbal game or puzzle? The options are practically infinite, but choose something short. Your person may enjoy five-hundred-page biographies of World War II generals, but do yourself a favor and take on something a little less ambitious.)

What genre will it be? (Romantic, silly, gothic, satirical?)

What will it be about?

When you've decided the form, genre or style, and subject, get started. Here are some examples of projects writers have created for their audiences of one:

- One wrote a humorous short story based on a *New Yorker* cartoon that his girlfriend liked.

- Another composed a song in the style of Gilbert and Sullivan for her father.

- One writer's sister wasn't a big reader but loved puzzles, so she created a verbal puzzle game out of lyrics from her sister's favorite songs.

Let the process of crafting a piece of writing with a specific recipient in mind be fun and rewarding.

When you finish, it's up to you whether or not you share the work with its intended audience. But either way, answer the following questions:

- Name at least three things you enjoyed about this.

- Name up to three aspects of this that were challenging for you.

- Did you stumble on anything you want to inject into your larger project? If so, what?

It's easy to get mired in the difficulty of a particular project or the ups and downs of the process and forget the ultimate goal of writing: to share it with someone whose life it will benefit. Keeping an idea in your mind of who your ideal reader is can help you stay focused on your vision and on why this project is important to you, why you started writing it in the first place.

"Should" is ultimately about ego—how you want others to see you as a writer, comparing yourself to particular writers who've come before you, an idea of your identity. The Trickster's job is to remind you to back off from that ego trip and remember to write what matters to you, not what you think others expect you to write.

Recapturing Play

Think about the very first piece of writing you ever invented. What was it: A story? A poem? A caption for a drawing? Mine was a page-long story I dictated to my father at age four that was, in retrospect, a pretty blatant rip-off of the picture book *Angelina Ballerina*, a favorite of mine at the time. I distinctly recall acting out the story with my toys on the floor while my father typed up my narration.

Writing begins as play. I wasn't "writing," or rather, I didn't know I was writing; to my mind, I was just playing. But playing often takes the form of storytelling.

Children don't say, "I'm going to play for three hours in the morning, four days a week." They play when given the opportunity; they invent and discard stories at will; and they play solely for their own entertainment.

A major focus of this book is on creating structures to help you meet your goals and do what you've set out to accomplish, and those structures can be extraordinarily helpful. But they can also choke the spontaneity and fun out of the experience of creative expression.

My client Lupe had been given a wonderful gift: a period of several months when she was able to focus solely on writing. At the beginning, worried she'd fritter away the time, she worked with me to create a structure she felt would keep her on track. She would revise her novel from 9 a.m. to 11 a.m., take a ten-minute break, then turn to a play script she was drafting from 11:10 a.m. to 1 p.m., and so on. Every day was scheduled down to the minute.

For a month or so, this worked well for her. She stuck to the schedule and got a lot accomplished.

Then it all started to fall apart. She was keeping to the schedule, but she stopped enjoying her work. Each block of time felt like a chore she had to get through. The less she wanted to be there, the more her writing suffered—and the harder it became for her to stick to the schedule. Soon, she was coming to our sessions miserable and stuck.

Talking it through, Lupe began to realize that she'd lost the sense of fun, of play, that made her love writing in the first place. The structure had worked initially, but it had become constricting to her creativity.

Lupe was reluctant to give up her system; for a while, it had worked better than anything she'd tried before, and going against it felt like cheating. But the rigidity of systems is in direct opposition to the fluidity of humanity. People evolve, grow, change, and as they do, so do their needs. Lupe needed to find a way to forgive herself for being human and allow herself to find new ways to address her new needs. She had to trust herself to continue to create *without* the training wheels of the rigid structure.

When Lupe at last gave herself permission to embark on this creative experiment, she broke all the rules she'd worked so hard to create. She used her time however she felt like, depending on the day. She wrote anything that took her fancy—or painted, or drew, or composed songs. When a wild train of thought came along, she followed it wherever it took her. Instead of making her art into work, she turned it into play, the way a child plays—creatively, spontaneously, and without imposed order or structure.

This playing allowed her to once again find enjoyment and fulfillment in her writing, which flourished.

In his book *The Power of Myth*, Joseph Campbell points to one of the oldest archetypal stories, that of Adam and Eve in the Garden of Eden, as an example of how a Trickster, the serpent, can upset an ordered world. Says Campbell, "No matter what the system of thought you may have, it can't possibly include boundless life. When you think everything is just that way, the trickster arrives, and it all blows, and you get change and becoming again."

Being a writer means making a certain number of rules for yourself. But in the middle of that structure—the goals you've set, the schedules you've made, the expectations you've built—it can be easy to lose the most natural, *fun* part of writing, the impulse that drives you to invent and imagine. Without that spark, your work may not only cease to be enjoyable, it can lose what makes it so uniquely *yours*.

Systems do work . . . for a while. Rules are useful . . . until they're not. You can go through this book diligently following the exercises and creating a structure for writing in your life, and that may serve you for a long time. But living beings thrive on change, and writing is a living being. The Trickster is here to remind us that, when we find the systems we've created are no longer of value, we are allowed to demolish them, like a child taking great delight in toppling a meticulously built tower of blocks, in order to build something fresh and new.

> *Systems do work . . . for a while. Rules are useful . . . until they're not.*

Pay close attention to how much the structures you've created are helping you. When you sit down to write at the times you've appointed for yourself, how do you feel? What about half an hour or an hour into your writing time? Do you continue to come up with fresh ideas and solutions that excite you, or are you feeling like you've lost that spark? Do you find yourself trudging through the work you've set out for yourself, but fantasizing about some other creative undertaking—a different writing project, or something else altogether?

Everybody has bad writing days, but if you find that, day after day, the work is utterly joyless, it may be time to give yourself a break and let your Trickster take over.

EXERCISE: PLAYING, NOT WRITING

This exercise is best suited to the moments when you're feeling burnt out on your project, when the process has grown stale, or when you're getting bored to death by your own seriousness. It's *not* a tool for procrastination, so save it for when you really need it.

Put down your pen, close your word processing program, and step away from your desk. For the next week, you're going to write without writing.

In the next seven days, do not work on your project. Give yourself a complete vacation from it.

Instead, we'll spend the time channeling your creative energies elsewhere. You will conceive of and create a brand-new work. There are unlimited possibilities for what you could make. Here are the only rules:

RULE #1: No writing allowed. No handwriting, no typing, no writing of any kind.

RULE #2: What you create must be ridiculous.

Here are a few suggestions to get you started:

- Make a video: a fake commercial, a pretend nature documentary, a soap opera of your own invention, a cat video starring humans as the cats . . .

- Create a musical in which all the characters are items found in your bathroom.

- Edit together scenes from your favorite movie or TV show to completely change what happens.

- Remember those "Magnetic Poetry Kits"? Create a piece of collaged writing made of scraps you've clipped from other sources (magazines, newspapers, discarded food packages found in your kitchen trash . . .).

- Put together a whole story just using gifs.

- Compose a song inspired by your favorite game.

Make this the only "writing" you do this week. Have fun!

We are capable of so much more than we restrict ourselves to. Comedian Jessica Delfino told me about a conversation she'd had with an artist friend about something the friend wanted to do that seemed daunting or difficult to Jessica. "You can do that?" Jessica asked, incredulous. Her friend replied, "Jessica, I'm an artist. I can do anything."

_____

We are capable of so much more than we restrict ourselves to.

_____

As children, we believe we can do anything, and as artists and writers, that remains true. The playful Trickster connects us to the part of ourselves that retains that capacity for endless possibility.

The Laughing Animal

According to humor scientist Scott Weems, humans laugh, on average, between fifteen and twenty times a day. Laughter is one of a limited number of involuntary actions—like sleeping, blinking, and relieving ourselves—that all humans perform daily. But these other actions are required in order to keep our bodies functioning properly; laughing isn't. So why has human evolution led us to develop laughter?

Nobody knows for sure, but there are plenty of theories. Neurologist V.S. Ramachandran argues that laughter is nature's way of signaling that a perceived threat is not actually dangerous, that it's a "false alarm." Laughter helps humans distinguish the grave from the benign, the real from the unreal. When we laugh, we are letting other humans know that they are not in danger.

We've all witnessed this in action when a toddler takes a tumble and, startled but not gravely injured, looks to the nearest adult for a sign of how to respond. If the adult rushes over exclaiming with worry and sympathy, the child tends to comply with tears; if the adult laughs, the child often easily moves on to the next activity. Before we can even talk, we understand what laughter means: *you're safe.*

Like writing, laughter is a form of communication and a way people connect with one another. Studies have shown that humans are more likely to be seen sharing laughter than any other emotional response.

Laughter, and by implication humor, is one of the strongest webs connecting people to one another.

Finding the Trickster within yourself gives you an important tool to mitigate the seriousness of your process and remind you of the foundations of writing. It's also crucial for navigating a world full of danger and alienation.

TV comedy writer Mehar Sethi told me a story that pulled back the curtain on "the writers' room," the inner sanctum in the office of every television show where the scripts are created. A veteran writer on shows like *The Cleveland Show*, *It's Always Sunny in Philadelphia*, and *BoJack Horseman*, Mehar described the writers' room to me as a raucous atmosphere in which humor is the only form of communication and bounces around like a ball from person to person. The conversation, he said, is "mostly about your sex life and lunch"—more tenth grade cafeteria table than Algonquin Round Table.

One day at one of the shows Mehar worked on, a writer came in with some heartbreaking news: his wife had miscarried. Not surprisingly, his way of dealing with pain was to turn it into humor, and his colleagues, wanting to cheer him up, joined in. The conversation escalated into the dirtiest, darkest barrage of terrible jokes that would never make it to television. The humor bridged the gulf between the writer and his colleagues, who shared his individual trauma. This sense of reconnection with his community did cheer him up. That is, until he realized he'd accidentally had his wife on speakerphone the entire time.

The illicit and Tricksterish thrill the writers felt from joking about such a deeply upsetting topic may have helped keep their fears about past or future traumatic experiences—like what their friend was going through—at bay. *If we're all laughing,* our deep programming tells us, *we can't be in real danger.*

The Trickster reminds us that so much of what we worry about in life is, in the grand scheme of things, not endangering our lives.

So while I hope you are taking this book seriously to a reasonable extent, I also encourage you to approach it—and your process—un-self-seriously, without heavy judgmental expectations on yourself, with playfulness and humor. Keep yourself entertained with your writing; if it doesn't entertain you, how will it captivate your audience? Don't forget that the work in which you're so deeply invested is, looked at from one angle, a massive prank that you're playing on your reader.

And if you grow frustrated that what you have labored to devise is not behaving as you intended—the piece itself, the structure you've built, your vision for your identity as a writer—remember the old saying: "Humans plan and God laughs."

Fail, but fail hilariously. In the midst of your own divine laughter, you'll find the strength to try again.

CHAPTER EIGHT

the goddess

identify your natural cycles
and make the most of them

Norman Mailer once said, "The problem is when you're not writing you don't know if you're lying fallow or if you'll never write again."

If someone as prolific and acclaimed as Mailer—someone who can win two Pulitzers *and* survive getting bashed in the head by Rip Torn wielding a hammer—felt this way, it's safe to surmise that every writer goes through this at some point. Sometimes, we are writing like mad and loving it; other times, often with little or no warning, we find our inspiration, creativity, and drive have simply dried up. And each time we lose our mojo, we feel like there's no way of knowing when or how—or if—we'll get it back.

I've witnessed these cycles in many writers, particularly those I've worked with for long periods of time. Some have a reliable ebb and flow—after several weeks of these writers showing up frustrated by a fallow phase, I can almost predict when they'll come to our session reenergized with some new idea. But more often, the cycles of writing are a bit like nature's seasons: we know spring will surely follow winter, and we have a general idea of the date range, but we're so uncertain beyond that, we look to a bucktoothed rodent and his shadow to tell us exactly when it'll happen each year.

In the life of any given writing project, we will go through seasons: periods of germination, creativity, reaping the fruits of our labors, and lying fallow. We cycle through these phases of letting an idea bubble beneath the surface, drafting it onto the page, molding that first effort into something more coherent, and taking a break from it, to get the clarity and perspective that sometimes only distance can provide.

We may struggle through certain seasons of the process, but without devoting time to each one, we cannot complete a project. For help with this, we turn to the archetype that embodies nature's cycles in the Hero's Journey: the **Goddess**.

> *In the life of any given writing project, we will go through seasons: periods of germination, creativity, reaping the fruits of our labors, and lying fallow.*

After facing several challenges on the journey, the Hero is granted a respite from conflict in the encounter with the Goddess. A symbol of the creativity and fertility in nature, the Goddess brings love to the Hero's life and reveals the Hero's own capacity to love. Through this, the Goddess helps the Hero see that everything in life has inherent cycles and that even the journey itself will come with its own ebbs and flows, episodes of fear and pain as well as moments of great joy and love. Through their encounter, the Hero discovers the creative wellspring within the self.

The Goddess, by the way, doesn't have to be a woman, or even a person. In ancient myths, the Hero is often a young man falling in love with a beautiful female Goddess. But in more contemporary stories, and in our lives, falling in love with the Goddess isn't necessarily a literal meeting of two people.

Whenever you participate in creation, whether you are making art, bringing a new life into the world, or starting a business or new venture, you are engaging in an act of connecting with the Goddess. Whenever you are affected by the sway of cycles on your life—the changing of the seasons, the rising and falling of the ocean's tide—that's the Goddess as well. Creativity thrives in the cradle of those cycles; the changes they bring are crucial to foster an environment for the nascent. Through our experience of these cycles, both their irresistibility and their constancy, the Goddess shows us their inherent potential for creation.

In this chapter, we'll address what season of the process you love best, and what season you struggle with the most. We'll look at what methods of working come naturally to you and find ways to make the most of them. And we'll examine how to get through those seasons of life when everything seems to be conspiring against your creative process.

Cycles of Nature

We are creatures of nature, and we exist in a natural world. Humans love to believe ourselves exempt from the rules that all other earthbound life-forms follow, but we are as much a part of nature as anything else is. The air we breathe, the water that sustains us, the ground in which we grow our nourishing crops, the rise and fall of the sun on whose light we depend—everything we need for our survival is dictated by nature's cycles.

Although most of us in the developed world no longer live as intimately with nature as earlier generations did, our brains still reflect these cycles. Neurologist and author Alice W. Flaherty explains that the human body, especially the brain, is inherently connected with these larger patterns. Our circadian rhythms reflect seasonal changes—as the nights get longer, our bodies recognize the approach of winter. While humans don't hibernate like bears, she says, "on average, people are less productive and less creative during the winter" and cites a study showing that artists tend to experience the biggest peak in productivity in early fall, followed by a smaller peak in the spring.

Humans are hard-wired for cycle. As a writer, you can fight this or you can use it to your advantage.

Women may be more familiar with the way nature's cycles show up in the body because of the egg's monthly joyride through our reproductive systems. Flaherty describes testosterone in men as "one long cycle"—instead of returning every thirty days, the cycle happens once, more gradually, over the course of a man's entire life.

Humans are hard-wired for cycle. As a writer, you can fight this or you can use it to your advantage.

One of the greatest sources of frustration I've witnessed in writers is when they're stuck in a season that they just don't like. Some feel most energized when they're germinating ideas and are loath to actually put anything on the page. Others are passionate about drafting; "If I actually had the time, I could sit here and write for eight or nine hours," one author told me. Still others crank through the first draft with gritted teeth, forcing themselves onward until they can relax into playing with the Rubik's cube of revision. While few writers I've met are happiest when not writing at all, stepping away from a project to give it breathing room can be a welcome relief.

Therapist and author Maureen Murdock writes about struggling to learn "the ability to move *with* the creative impulse without trying to force it" when it comes to the natural cycles of work and life. It's easier said than done. The Goddess is a tool we can use to embrace the seasons of the process—to find patience to endure the seasons we dislike, and to extract value from all of them and see all of them as reflections of our varied gifts.

EXERCISE: TO EVERYTHING THERE IS A SEASON

the hero is you

Use this exercise when you're uncertain where you sit in the year of your writing life, or to identify which season you're experiencing.

Here, the four seasons of the year represent four major phases of the writing process.

Spring: Thinking of a new idea for a project.

Summer: Putting your thoughts down on the page in a first draft.

Autumn: Gathering and shaping those thoughts into a more polished version.

Winter: Taking a break from a project in order to come back refreshed.

Create a pie chart with four sections in your journal and label the sections "Spring," "Summer," "Autumn," and "Winter." For each of the following questions that you answer "yes" to, put the appropriate symbol in the matching season. (That is, if you answer "yes" to a question with a leaf beside it, put a leaf in the Spring section of the pie.)

- Have you gotten an idea for a new project within the past week? 🍃

- Is part of the pleasure of writing, for you, the feeling of returning to it after an absence? ❄

- When a new idea comes to you, do you like to start writing right away? 🌸

- Do you write messy first drafts that dump all your thoughts out on the page? 🌼

- Do you feel more comfortable once you have a draft down and something to work with? 🍎

- Have you had at least three ideas for new projects in the past three months? 🍃

- Do you feel good about stepping away from your work to clear your head for a few days, weeks, or even months? ❄️

- When writer friends need someone to edit their work, do they often call on you? 🍎

- Do you enjoy doing research to find out more about the subjects you're writing about before diving in? 🍃

- When you put a project on the back burner for a while, do you jump right into drafting another piece you've been thinking about? 🌼

- When you get feedback on your work, are you excited to apply it? 🍎

- Can you usually tell when it's time to take a break from a project and give it some air? ❄️

- Once you start revising, do you find it difficult to know when to stop? 🍎

- Do you love telling stories that you make up on the spot? 🌼

- Do you enjoy having periods of time when you don't write? ❄️

- When you get an idea for a new project, do you like to let it simmer for a while? 🍃

- When writing a first draft, could you keep going for hours on end? 🌼

- Do you find that, no matter how passionate you are about writing, sometimes it's just not where you want to focus your energy? ❄️

- If you get bored or stuck with a project you're working on, do you find you suddenly come up with your best-ever brand-new idea for something totally unrelated? 🍃

When you've answered all the questions, look at the diagram to see which section is the most full. You may find that more than one is equally filled.

If Spring is full of leaves . . .

You are deeply connected with your Herald and love getting inspired and generating new ideas. Spring is all about new beginnings, tender shoots and buds appearing for the first time, and your greatest passion in the writing process is in seeing these buds of ideas emerge. You might struggle to stay focused on a long-haul project, because you're easily distracted by the latest and greatest.

If Summer is full of flowers . . .

There's nothing you love more than rolling up your sleeves and letting your fingers fly across the page or keyboard. If left to your own devices, you might forget to eat or go to the bathroom—that's how much you love filling up the page. Like a child in a folktale who wanders too far picking wildflowers and stumbles upon a wolf or a fairy ring, you can run the risk of rambling so far afield from your original idea that when you step back from your draft, it doesn't completely make sense. But that's okay—you'd rather blurt it all out and have fun doing it, and worry about fixing it up later.

If Autumn is full of apples . . .

Drafting isn't your favorite, but once you've got something on the page to work with, you get to strut your stuff. A master reviser, you love the challenge of turning that first draft into a polished work—it's like taking all the ingredients you threw on the page and corralling them, with precision, into a pie. You may fight your way through that first draft process, because you have to rein in your Threshold Guardians and remind yourself that the writing doesn't have to be perfect. But nothing satisfies you more than when the piece finally looks as good, or nearly as good, as you envisioned it in your head.

If Winter is full of snowflakes . . .

You aren't an every-day writer, or even an every-week writer, and you're okay with that. Writing's role in your life is important, but it's not the only important thing to you—plus, sometimes it really drives you crazy—and you recognize the value of stepping away from it. It can be scary not knowing when you'll return to it. But you know that even when your writing is dormant, germination is happening under the soil, and that when the next bud of an idea peeks its head up, it will be more fully formed than had you rushed it to light.

Now look at which section or sections are the sparsest. This will show you which season(s) you feel least comfortable with or connected to, at least right now.

Write down which one you're having the hardest time with.

Keep this season in mind throughout the rest of the chapter, as we'll look at ways to use your natural rhythms to address that struggle.

Writing Versus Typing

Shannon emailed me before our coaching session, as she always did, with her agenda of what she planned to discuss. That week, the list only had one item on it: "I'm in a rut!"

When we'd spoken just two weeks before, she'd been excited about the new novel she'd recently begun working on. But on our call, Shannon sounded frustrated and gloomy and berated herself for not writing. All she was doing, she explained with disgust, was researching the historical era of her novel, reading published novels with similar settings, and creating dozens of notecards with information about the characters she was developing.

I finally broke in and told her, "I don't think you're in a rut. You're writing; you're just not *typing*." Everything she was doing was part of the writing process. Not only was she not in a rut, she was working her butt off. She just couldn't see it, because to her, "writing" meant drafting.

The first step toward a more fulfilling experience of writing is opening your mind to the seasons of the process and being willing to see each stage as writing, even when you're not actively generating words. Even Winter is an act of writing—without taking time away from a piece, the rest of the process would be impossible.

This may sound simple, but it's something I see writers overlook all the time. I spoke with screenwriter Lexie Kahanovitz a month after she'd gone into production on the TV pilot she'd been writing and revising for the past three years. Her longtime dream was finally being realized—she was turning her script into a television show with actors, sets, animation, and music. Best of all, she was producing it, so she had total control. Yet the first thing she said when I asked her how it was going was, "I'm worried because I feel like I haven't written for a long time."

Production is writing. Research is writing. Workshopping is writing, revising is writing, studying the work of your idols is writing, pausing to clear your head is writing. Anything that serves the work—that isn't a distractive task cooked up by a Threshold Guardian instead—is writing.

Of course, understanding this is one thing; internalizing it is another matter. Writers trapped in an unappealing season of the process can often fall prey to a kind of fatalism not unlike people in the grip of depression, who find it impossible to remember feeling any other way or to believe that circumstances will ever change.

But nothing is more inevitable than change. As spring always follows winter, as day always follows night, each phase of your writing process always, eventually, yields to the next. And each time you cycle through, you grow in experience and wisdom.

Nothing is more inevitable than change.

As Rilke said, "Being an artist means: not numbering and counting, but ripening like a tree, which doesn't force its sap, and stands confidently in the storms of spring, not afraid that afterward summer may not come."

The best ways to resist fatalism is to collect as much information as you can about your own inherent cycles. When you have a sense of what to expect, you're less likely to get stymied. This starts with paying attention to the patterns you find yourself naturally following, sometimes without even realizing you're doing it.

Know Thyself

Author MacKenzie Cadenhead was an editor at Marvel Comics before shifting gears to focus on writing fiction. When she worked on her first novel, then her second, she noticed a pattern beginning to emerge in her process. The first third of her draft always developed on the page very slowly because every time she sat down, she'd go back and revise everything she'd already written. She knew striving for that level of polish in a first draft was impractical, but something kept driving her to work and rework the beginning of the novel.

Eventually, she'd hit a wall of self-recrimination: *What am I doing? Why is this taking me so long?* But once she pushed past that barrier, she suddenly felt free to write much more sloppily and stop editing herself, and she could complete the rest of the draft without ever pausing to go back and edit.

MacKenzie initially fought against these tendencies by trying to make herself stop editing that first third and crank through, but it was a tremendous battle. When she noticed the pattern repeating, she began to consider more deeply where it might be coming from.

Looking back, she realized that it was the same pattern she'd gone through for years when editing comic books. The comic books she worked on were serial, so for the first few issues of each new series, she'd keep the writers on a tight editorial leash to make sure they gave the series a solid start. She had them create a "beat sheet" listing all the plot points in the book, sometimes down to a page-by-page level, because she needed to be able to weigh in on even the smallest flaw in the storytelling. But by the third issue, when she felt confident the writers had a handle on the characters and where the story needed to go, she relaxed her grip and let them plow ahead and write the script without running a detailed outline by her first.

Now she was treating herself as if she were one of the writers she had edited. When she saw her pattern through this lens, she understood why that first third was so tough for her. Like in the comic books she had supervised, she believed a solid, thoughtfully constructed foundation was essential to building the rest of the work. Having a strong beginning was also an emotional support tool for her; if something went haywire later on in the manuscript, she could always go back to the first third and persuade herself that, in her words, "the book isn't total shit." Crafting a tight first third gave her the confidence boost she needed to get the rest of the draft onto the page.

"I had to accept that this is who I am," she told me. "The editor and writer have to both be there at the start, and then the writer can go and run for a while and vomit it out."

MacKenzie asked herself where the pattern was coming from, recognized its source in her life, assessed how the pattern was serving her work, and going forward, flowed with it and used it to help her rather than fighting against it.

Every writer has a natural work rhythm—in general and for each specific project. You might find that, like MacKenzie, you have patterns you always fall into, or you may discover that each project brings you a totally new work cycle.

Every writer has a natural work rhythm—in general and for each specific project.

Stand-up comedian Myq Kaplan preserves all his ideas on a digital recorder and then transcribes them, first in longhand, then typed. He's discovered that his natural way to produce his best work is this tri-part process—"I say it, I write it, I type it," he told me—and he loves working this way. Anything that isn't funny enough or just doesn't work falls away in translating from recorded speech to handwritten words and from notebook to computer, leaving him with the work he feels best about. But even after he's put a comedy bit through these filters, he wouldn't call it "done" until he's had the chance to speak it aloud again, this time in front of an audience.

The habits and cycles you find yourself naturally drawn to can be a valuable tool to help you be your most productive and reduce your frustration. What they should *not* become is an excuse to not do the work.

I can't tell you how many writers have explained to me why they're not writing more by listing all the things they simply *can't* do: "Oh, I can't write at night." "I can only write when nobody else is in the house." "I need at least three hours set aside to get any writing done." Any of that sound familiar?

When it comes to writing, we *can* do just about anything we set our minds to. Miguel de Cervantes wrote part of *Don Quixote* in prison; Laura Hillenbrand penned her bestsellers *Seabiscuit* and *Unbroken* in bed while chronically ill. Jean-Dominique Bauby, whose entire body was paralyzed by a stroke, wrote his famed memoir *The Diving Bell and the Butterfly* a single letter at a time by signaling with his left eyelid to his assistant who read the alphabet aloud for him over and over. Those with the unquenchable thirst for self-expression can find a way to write no matter what the circumstances. If it is truly your fervent desire to write, no excuse justifies not writing at all.

That being said, for those of us who strive to create a regular writing practice that is productive and keeps us in an emotionally healthy frame of mind, knowing our natural tendencies—such as what time of day we are usually at our sharpest or how long we can write on any given day before reaching mental burnout—can be extremely valuable. By using your natural predilections to build a practice on, you can stop feeling subject to them and harness them to help you.

There are writers who are most clearheaded first thing in the morning and writers who do their best work late at night. Author Ann Beattie once said that no matter what time she got out of bed in the morning, she felt as if she'd just woken up, and preferred to write between midnight and three a.m. Günter Grass said he didn't believe in writing at night at all. Richard Wright worked up to fifteen hours at a time when writing *Native Son*, while Gertrude Stein never wrote more than half an hour a day. Anthony Trollope commenced at five-thirty every morning and claimed he'd trained himself to write 250 words every fifteen minutes for three hours. Umberto Eco has said it would be "impossible" for him to follow a schedule. Jane Austen wrote in her family's very social sitting room; Maya Angelou could only concentrate by renting a hotel room, to which she'd bring a dictionary, a Bible, a deck of cards, and a bottle of sherry.

You might find you can get the most accomplished by sitting down for large time blocks, or you may prefer working in shorter bursts. You might discover that sitting down to write every day at the same time makes you most productive, or you may find that two or three days a week allow you to focus more keenly (the idea that every "real" writer "should" write every day is definitely a myth). You might prefer to write in solitude or you may find it helpful to have others nearby while you work.

The more information you have about what your own naturally occurring habits are, the easier it will be to build a structure for your writing practice that works and feels good.

EXERCISE: PRACTICE MIX-AND-MATCH

If you already have a good sense of when and how you do your best work, great. If not, or if you suspect you could be more productive or find a happier way to work, this exercise is for you.

Using the columns below, choose one item from each category to create what you currently believe your best practices to be.

Time of Day	Frequency in Week	Regularity	Amount of Time in Day	Environment	Allies
Morning	Every day	Very regular schedule (always at same times)	1 chunk of 3–5 hours	At home in a quiet room alone	With an Ally also writing
Afternoon	Weekdays		2 chunks of 1–2 hours	At home with people around	With an Ally doing nonwriting work
Evening	3 days				
Late-night	1 day	Varied schedule (different days, different times)	3 chunks of 30 minutes–1 hour	Out of the home somewhere solitary	Without an Ally
Varied times			More than 3 chunks of 5–30 minutes	Out of the home in a peopled environment	

Now, put what you think is your best method into practice.

For example, let's say you chose this combination:

Morning, three days a week, very regular schedule, one chunk of three to five hours, out of the home in a peopled environment, with an Ally also writing.

This week, set aside three days to write for three to five hours each day at the same time in the morning. Make a plan with an Ally, or more than one for different days if needed, to go somewhere—a coffee shop, a restaurant, a public park, the library, wherever you prefer—and write.

At the end of the week, answer the following questions:

- Each day, how long did it take you to get started?

- How many days were you able to get into a flow state?

- Based on what you hoped to accomplish this week, would you say you didn't meet your goals, nearly met your goals, met your goals, or exceeded your goals?

- One a scale of one to ten, one being miserable and ten being happy and fulfilled, how do you feel about being a writer this week?

- Would you like to work this way again?

The following week, choose a different combination. Don't pick any of the same factors—for example, you might try *varied times, weekdays, varied schedule, 3 chunks of 30 min–1 hour, at home in a quiet room alone, without an Ally.* For one week, see how this goes for you. At the end of the week, answer the same questions.

Keep repeating with different combinations until you find the one that seems to work the best for you—at least for now. Nature is ever-changing, and so are you!

Life Cycles

We can channel the power of the Goddess to ride through the seasons of the writing process, create a structure that honors our natural habits, and rigorously pursue our own best ways of working with each new project. And just when it seems we've gotten it all figured out, life changes again and we have to start all over.

Ruth McKee had been a working playwright for fifteen years. She'd had plays produced all over the country, cofounded a theater company called Chalk Repertory Theatre in Los Angeles, and taught playwriting at the college level at various universities. When she wasn't busy with any of those, she was reading scripts for theater companies, meeting with her various writers' groups, and sending her work out to theaters and grant committees for consideration.

Her life revolved around her writing career. But everything was thrown askew when she and her husband became parents.

Having a child didn't impact her writing career right away. When her first, a son, was born, Ruth was prepared—she already had many plays in various stages of development, and during her baby's first year of life, saw several productions of her work put on across the country.

When her son was two years old and her daughter six months, though, Ruth became increasingly aware that, while she'd seen all those projects through, she hadn't generated any new work in the past two years. And with a toddler and an infant to care for, she wasn't likely to anytime soon.

Ruth and her husband, also a writer, had always worked in opposite styles. Before parenthood, Ruth had typically written two or three days per week, while her husband, screenwriter and comic book author Brian K. Vaughan, wrote every day. Brian's work, often science fiction, came largely from his imagination, while Ruth's realist works were typically inspired by current events and drew on the people and places she saw and experienced. The couple had grown accustomed to Brian's need for solitude and Ruth's need for social interaction to feed their respective writing.

Having children made Ruth's writing even less frequent, and Brian's more urgent. It had never bothered Ruth that as a playwright, her work was the less lucrative of the pair, as long as she'd been able to find ways to support herself. But now writing *cost* money—if she wanted to write, she had to pay a sitter. Brian, who'd written on the staff of *Lost* and other TV shows in addition to creating comic books, now had to choose projects more strategically, with an eye to what could support their family in the long term.

Faced with the financial reality of their situation and looking at the price tag of raising two children in Los Angeles, Ruth found herself asking, *Is writing plays what I should be doing with my life?* Post-BFA and MFA, she wondered if she'd spent all these years becoming a specialist in the wrong area, one that wouldn't even allow her to support her family. Had it all been a big mistake?

Many artists—whether they're also juggling parenthood or not—find themselves asking these questions, especially between their midthirties and early forties. Ruth had laid out a career path at nineteen that she'd been trying to follow ever since, and at this moment, she felt she'd failed. She wasn't where she'd envisioned herself being by age thirty-four, and now she was considering abandoning the career she'd been building since college.

It was that or adjust her expectations. She chose the latter.

Ruth decided to start by cutting anything unessential from her days. She stopped submitting her work widely in the "spray and pray" method she'd been using since she'd bought the *Dramatists Sourcebook* in college. She resigned from the theater where she'd been volunteering to read scripts. She quit all her writing groups apart from one. She stopped accepting low-paying teaching gigs, which she'd taken in the past mainly to get the experience, and accepted only those that were financially worth the time.

When she eliminated all this from her schedule, she was left with two elements to her writing life: Chalk Rep, which remained her artistic home, and the writing itself. She didn't want to abandon Chalk Rep. And, having cut everything else out, she found she didn't want to stop writing.

It hadn't all been a mistake. Ruth McKee was a writer. She was also a mother. She could do both—but not by following rules she'd made as a teenager. She had to redefine her writing career, at least for now. She knew that, once her kids were old enough to be in school, it would all change again—not back to the way it had been before, but by continuing to evolve.

Ruth's experience exemplifies the large-scale cycles our lives can pull us into. We may have periods of several years when life doesn't sustain our writing the way it once did. That doesn't mean we have to throw out writing entirely or forever—but it does mean making some major adjustments.

Parenting and writing are challenging to balance, but eventually, Ruth said to me, "Children grow up to become people you have interesting conversations with, see the world through. They ultimately enrich your life as a creative person." She'd always sought social interactions for inspiration; now her children were providing a new kind. Likewise, other life cycles that can take us away from writing—caring for ailing or elderly relatives, following other professional opportunities, health crises of our own, involvement in social or political movements, to name a few—can, in the long run, enrich our writing and deepen our empathy and our humanity.

All writers are enmeshed in an endless spiral, returning to the page again and again, each time bringing to the process all we have drawn from our most recent life experiences to infuse into our work.

Maureen Murdock talks about a distinction that has been made between feminine and masculine creativity—that feminine tends to spiral whereas masculine tends to move forward linearly. But all writers are enmeshed in an endless spiral, returning to the page again and again, each time bringing to the process all we have drawn from our most recent life experiences to infuse into our work. No matter how long our hiatus may be from writing, the curving line of the spiral will inevitably bring us back to it.

As in all love affairs, the Hero and the Goddess must eventually part ways. But the Hero leaves the encounter changed—the experience of loving, and being loved, unlocks a part of the Hero that had previously been latent. In a sense, the Hero takes the Goddess and her creativity, mastery of cycles, and boundless love along on the next stage of the journey, where all three will be much needed.

As the writing journey continues, we ride through the cycles of the process and of life, finding that love is all around, within and without.

CHAPTER NINE

the shadow

fight the destructive impulse and discover your hidden power

When he was nineteen years old, Brian Herrera stopped writing.

Just two years earlier, he'd been one of the most vaunted young writers in the country. As a high school senior, he'd entered a patriotic speech-writing contest called "The Voice of Democracy Scholarship Program" on a whim and won first place out of 300,000 entries. The honor led to the strangest, most exhilarating five months of his life, including a trip to Washington, D.C., delivering his speech to an audience of 3,500 at the Annual Congressional Banquet, and hobnobbing with senators, congressional representatives, and the media. He'd come out of the experience with greater confidence in his writing's ability to get him anything, including a full ride to college, not to mention a handful of great stories to tell at cocktail parties for the rest of his life.

But two years later, he abruptly quit. And he didn't write again for fifteen years.

What stopped him? The **Shadow**.

Building the Shadow, Brick by Brick

In the Hero's Journey, the Shadow is the antagonist whose efforts to thwart the Hero make up the primary conflict of the story. Whatever stands in a Hero's way, whether it takes the form of another character, a repressive government, or even just a perceived limitation in the protagonist's own psyche, is the Shadow.

Carl Jung coined the term "Shadow" to describe the side of ourselves that we hide away in the dark corners of our psyches. Communities and even whole societies can have their own Shadows, collective pools of guilt, shame, or fear that these groups repress and pass along to generation after generation.

But Shadows are more than just sources of pain and conflict in the lives of the Heroes they seek to thwart. They challenge Heroes to train, study, marshal Allies, and tap their deepest reserves of intelligence, ability, and courage in order to battle them. They push Heroes to face their own dark sides. By threatening Heroes with the specter of death, they give those Heroes the opportunity to be reborn as someone new.

Whatever stands in a Hero's way, whether it takes the form of another character, a repressive government, or even just a perceived limitation in the protagonist's own psyche, is the Shadow.

In the Hero's Journey of your writing process, you have—or will—come face-to-face with a Shadow of your own. This isn't like the aggravating Threshold Guardians that prevent you from focusing on any given day. The Guardians represent distraction; the Shadow represents destruction.

After Brian had delivered his speech at the banquet in Washington, an elderly senator had approached him, eyes shining warmly. He exuded, in Brian's description, a "glow" of celebrity—he was clearly used to everyone knowing who he was, though his name meant nothing to a seventeen-year-old kid from New Mexico. The senator shook Brian's hand.

"My office could use a writer like you," he told Brian in a gentle Southern twang. "You come on down from that college next summer, young man, and you write me a speech or two, just like the one you just read. This country needs more young people like you."

Brian was flattered, proud that he'd inspired such a response from someone clearly well respected and powerful. It wasn't until two years later, as a college sophomore sitting in a lecture on twentieth-century American history, that Brian heard the senator's name again and realized exactly whom his speech had so inspired.

The senator who'd enthusiastically offered Brian a summer job had opposed granting civil rights to African American citizens with such vigor that he'd quit the Democratic Party, written the Southern Manifesto protesting *Brown v. Board of Education*, run for president on a platform centered around preserving the Jim Crow laws, and conducted what remains the longest filibuster by any individual American senator (twenty-four hours and eighteen minutes)—oh yeah, and he'd fathered a daughter with his family's black maid.

Brian's biggest fan was Senator Strom Thurmond.

"Right then, right there, I decided that I was not to be trusted with the written word," Brian said later. "I decided to hold close to my words, to keep them in my mouth, to keep them in the moment. Writing them down was too risky."

Only nineteen years old, still figuring out what it meant to be a gay man in the late 1980s and a Latino man in the United States, Brian became frozen with fear about the potential his writing had to hold meanings he hadn't intended, to be appreciated and even used by people beyond his control—like, say, a senator who had tried to smear Martin Luther King by intimating that the civil rights leader was involved with his openly gay speechwriter, Bayard Rustin, called disparagingly by Thurmond a "communist, draft-dodger, and homosexual."

"From this moment," Brian said, "I started carefully stacking the bricks of the writer's block that would eventually nearly ruin me."

The Shadow is the force that halts your work—not just for a day or two, but for an extended, painful period of time. Unlike the "Winter" we discussed in the Goddess chapter—an organic hiatus from a specific project—the Shadow represents a total writing shutdown. And unlike the Threshold Guardians—distractive tendencies that we can, with the right technique, push past on any given day—the Shadow is a deeper, more chronic destructive impulse against your work.

Like a witch in a fairy tale who feeds off youth and beauty, the Shadow is rooted in the vulnerabilities you already possess, like low confidence, anger, depression, and anxiety, whether clinically diagnosed or simply a part of your psyche's particular mix. Combine a tendency toward any of these conditions with a heavy roadblock in your writing and you are looking at a Shadow.

Since writing and life are engaged in a constant dialogue, sources of pain in our lives can alienate us from our work. I've seen many Shadows, like Brian's, emerge from the chemical reaction of a traumatic experience with feedback (often criticism, but in this case, praise from an unwanted quarter), colliding with preexisting fears and insecurities, not just about writing but about oneself.

When Brian began to fear his own writing, Strom Thurmond—or, more accurately, a Strom Thurmond-faced character Brian created, representing evil, exploitation, and manipulation—became a part of his inner landscape, and with a disproportionate amount of power: the power to stop him from creating his own work. Perhaps there's someone in your life whose face you've used to costume a deeply held fear or insecurity, whose voice you hear in your head and has the power to halt your writing. Everyone's Shadow shows up in a different form, but what they all share is an ability to stand between you and your work.

Everyone's Shadow shows up in a different form, but what they all share is an ability to stand between you and your work.

In the pages that follow, we'll be visiting a dark place: the source of what most holds you back in your writing. We will shine a light on that Shadow, taking concrete steps to steal its power and turn it into a source of motivation and confidence in your work and life.

A word about the exercises in this chapter: they are intended to help you extract yourself from a severe estrangement from writing. If you're not currently experiencing this, I recommend reserving them for a future time when you may be in that situation, when they can be most helpful to you. I only use these with writers who have addressed all other possible obstacles to writing—getting distracted, not having enough time, lacking direction—and are still finding themselves unable to write. The general content of the chapter, though, can be relevant any time.

EXERCISE: SNAPSHOT OF YOUR SHADOW

At the root of most Shadows is fear. This exercise aims to identify what you are afraid of that has spawned this Shadow blocking your path.

Imagine you have just woken up from a terrible nightmare in which you lived out the worst possible scenario with regards to your writing. (I don't mean an externally imposed scenario, like your computer, with your entire completed manuscript saved on it, slips out of your arms and settles on the floor of Lake Michigan where a water snake turns it into a nest. I mean a scenario that's a result of your actions—the screenplay you wrote is finally produced to huge fanfare and it's a complete disaster, with all of Hollywood mocking you as a failure, or you try and try but never manage to get so much as a single poem published for the rest of your life. You get the idea.)

Write out the dream as you imagine it.

Based on the events of the nightmare, complete the following phrase:

My greatest fear is . . .

(For example, "I'll never be a good enough writer to succeed"; "other people will think my work is stupid"; "it's already too late for me to start a writing career.")

Now rephrase this fear or challenge as an accusing statement. (For example, "You'll never be a good enough writer to succeed"; "If you share your work with others, they'll laugh at you"; "You're totally undisciplined and can't stick to your commitments.")

the shadow

This is your Shadow talking.

What kind of person or creature would say this to you? Let's find out.

Fill out the following Character Sheet for your Shadow.

Some prompts to get you started:

- What does this Shadow look like?

- What kind of personality does this Shadow have—mocking, deadly serious, dismissive?

- Draw inspiration from fiction, history, and people in your own life. Is your Shadow a Disney witch, a Kafkaesque bureaucrat, a sinister mobster, your tenth grade English teacher—or some blend or mashup?

Create an image of your Shadow.

NAME: What is your Shadow's name?

DESCRIPTION: Give a brief description of your Shadow.

SKILLS: List the ways your Shadow hampers you.

We'll return to this, and flesh it out more, later in the chapter.

Origin Stories

In Germany in the late 1920s, a little Jewish boy named Max was born. Growing up under the Nazis' rise to power, he witnessed his family and his community suffer terrible discrimination. After fleeing to Poland, his mother, father, and sister were executed while Max hid in their mass grave. Eventually, he was sent to Auschwitz, where he was forced to work helping the Nazis operate the gas chambers of the camp. While a prisoner there, Max reunited with a girl he'd known as a child and they fell in love, and eventually fled the camp together during a revolt. But Max's experiences of prejudice didn't end there, and eventually led to the death of his daughter and wife and forced him to, once again, run for his life, this time to Israel, where he met a man named . . . Charles Xavier.

If you didn't already figure it out, Max—or Magneto, as he came to be known—is a fictional supervillain who takes the Shadow role in the X-Men comic books. His goal is to overthrow society and claim the world for mutants, even if it means destroying all humans in the process. To the X-Men, he is a menace who must be stopped. But from Magneto's perspective, he's trying to prevent mutants like himself from being persecuted, at any cost. Knowing he spent his childhood and young adulthood experiencing the most brutal persecution humankind could muster, it's hard to blame him for distrusting humans and wishing to protect his people from such atrocities. His actions, unchecked, could mean the end of human life on Earth—but he believes he's doing good.

The impulse to stop writing often comes out of fear, but at the root of that fear may be an altruistic intention. In Brian Herrera's case, his paralysis stemmed from a deep-seated belief that his writing possessed a power he couldn't control—that if released onto the page, it could perform independent actions, like inspiring a powerful man whose values were completely antithetical to Brian's. At the core of that belief was an older, deeper fear: that Brian could not trust himself.

Whether he was conscious of this or not at the time, Brian held a core belief that, as long as he didn't write, he wouldn't be endorsing or aiding the Strom Thurmonds of the world. Stopping writing was, in his mind, the only effective and responsible way to rein himself in and prevent the inevitable damage he'd do the world if left unchecked.

It's possible the force that stops you in your writing tracks came directly from someone deliberately trying to sabotage and hurt you. But it's much more likely that your Shadow developed out of good intentions, a little voice in your head that is modeled on a parent or teacher who was trying to protect you from suffering, or your own desire to do what you perceived as the right thing. Like Brian, you may have been afraid of the power your words could hold, or the way they might be interpreted once you release them. Or like Magneto, you might have been trying to shield yourself from some past misery you never want to experience again.

My client Joan grew up in a home where creativity was discouraged and being artistic was seen as weakness. Most likely, her parents weren't deliberately trying to be cruel—they probably just wanted, as many parents do, to ensure their children would have secure, stable lives, and to them that meant squashing artistic dreams.

Of course, this ended up having the opposite effect, and when Joan left home, she became an acid-tripping, free-loving hippie. But for years, she remained afraid to write, paint, or draw because whenever she picked up her pen or paintbrush, she was like a dog trapped inside an invisible fence, feeling the *zap* of her Shadow, a voice inside that told her not to waste her time trying to make art. Still afraid of being wounded by her parents' criticism, even long after their deaths, she was prevented by this self-protective impulse from doing what she loved.

But being protected wasn't helping or shielding her; it was holding her back.

What old voices might still be echoing in your psyche? What part of yourself might you have developed to protect your heart from anticipated pain? How might you be doing a Magneto on yourself—destroying in the name of preserving?

EXERCISE: ORIGIN STORIES

In this exercise, we'll investigate your Shadow to identify how it developed and what, if anything, it might have been protecting you from.

Using the Shadow you described in the previous exercise, we're going to create an imagined interview. You can interview your Shadow as yourself, or you can have a character do it for you. You might use a (real or imagined) TV talk show host, investigative reporter, psychiatrist or therapist, gossip blogger, even a life coach, or something else entirely. Consider what sort of person/profession would be most ideally suited to get to the heart of your Shadow's backstory from a place of love, not judgment. This interviewer isn't here to condemn your Shadow—just to listen.

I've provided some questions to use as a jumping-off point, but feel free to go off script with your own queries for your Shadow.

Interviewer: (examples: Oprah, Anderson Cooper, David Frost, yourself)

Format: (examples: prime-time TV show, therapy session, dictating memoirs to ghostwriter)

INTERVIEWER: [Shadow's name], thank you so much for joining me today. I'm really looking forward to getting to know more about you.

SHADOW: . . .

INTERVIEWER: Let's begin with the basics. When and where were you born?

SHADOW: . . .

INTERVIEWER: What was [reader's name]'s life like before you came along?

SHADOW: . . .

INTERVIEWER: How did things change for [reader's name] when you appeared?

SHADOW: . . .

INTERVIEWER: What one moment would you pinpoint as defining who you are as a Shadow?

SHADOW: . . .

INTERVIEWER: Why do you think [reader] shouldn't write?

SHADOW: . . .

INTERVIEWER: If you could give one gift to [reader], what would it be?

SHADOW: . . .

INTERVIEWER: What is your raison d'être? What gets you out of bed in the morning?

SHADOW: . . .

INTERVIEWER: What is your exact opposite?

SHADOW:. . .

[add your own questions]

INTERVIEWER: Well, this has been fascinating. Thank you so much for joining us today! My guest has been [Shadow's name].

When you're done, read over the interview and see what your Shadow has shared about how it developed, what sources of pain it may have been trying to protect you from, and what role it performs in your life today.

Summarize the most valuable/interesting/surprising take-aways from the interview by completing these three sentences:

- My Shadow came from . . .

- My Shadow wanted/wants to protect me from . . .

- What is still useful about my Shadow is . . .

Now that you've identified and investigated your Shadow's origin and motivations, you're mere steps away from taking away its power over your life.

Talking to the Dark

After deciding not to write, Brian focused his energies on his other gift: the theater. He spent the next fifteen years working hard at establishing a career as a director and professor of theater studies. He was good at directing, he loved the theater environment, and he liked the work fine. But it didn't spark his passion the way writing had.

It was the opening night of one of the shows he'd directed. As Brian stood backstage a few minutes before the curtain went up, corralling actors, giving last-minute notes, and checking with the stage manager that all was set to go, Brian caught himself wishing he were at home writing.

Something in him snapped. If he couldn't get passionate about directing at one of the most thrilling moments of the job—if, even in the lion's mouth, he'd rather be writing—what was he doing with his life?

He knew he had to start writing again. The only way to begin after so long was to tell the story he had to purge from his system: the story of being the Voice of Democracy.

Over the next five years, Brian began, little by little, to circle around this story without quite writing it. Then, a friend of his who was running a workshop on live storytelling was short one student and begged Brian to participate. He really didn't want to, but the university where he taught had given him a budget that he needed to spend down before the end of the year or he'd lose it. Rather than see the money go to waste, he decided to spend it on the workshop.

He had never imagined the workshop would lead him to write the full story or that his fellow participants would encourage him to submit it to a local festival or that *I Was the Voice of Democracy* would be so popular, Brian would be asked to give the encore performance of the festival. That festival led to more and more requests for him to perform his piece, and the more he did it, the more feedback he received and the better it got.

Brian's fear of being vulnerable had prevented him from writing, but in the end, allowing himself to be vulnerable, and offering his audiences empathy about their own fears—getting up in front of friends and strangers, night after night, and telling them the story of why he'd spent fifteen years afraid to write—finally destroyed his Shadow.

Since then, Brian has presented countless performances of *I Was the Voice of Democracy* in cities across the country including New York, Los Angeles, and Seattle, at national conferences, on public radio, and internationally in Beirut and Abu Dhabi.

And he has continued to write.

Shadows, by their very name, thrive in the dark. When we try to lock away the source of our frustration and pain, out of shame or fear, we allow it to gain power. But when we give it a face and a name—as in the previous exercises—and instead of trying to hide it in the basement of our psyches, bring it out into the light, its hold over us often ebbs away.

Fighting Back

There is no single "right" or "best" way to deal with your Shadow, and what works for you today may be different from what helps you in the future. You may encounter the Shadow more than once over the years, and the source of each Shadow may be different and may require different solutions.

Any one of the points below could be the inspiration for an exercise, but I can't fit them all into this book. So let these prompts inspire exercises of your own devising, as jumping-off points to lead you into combat with your own particular Shadow.

MINDFULNESS

With the clinical interest of a scientist doing an experiment, pay close attention to your Shadow's habits without judgment. Don't try to change your behavior yet. Simply notice what makes your Shadow flare up and what makes it die down. When do you struggle the most with writing? Is that struggle cyclical, and if so, what precipitates the cycle? Is something happening in your life outside of writing that triggers you to feel blocked, stuck, or despondent in your work?

Just placing awareness on your Shadow can be an effective first step toward addressing it.

TALKING

One of my clients froze up when she was two chapters away from completing her first manuscript and didn't realize that a paralyzing fear of failure was stopping her from finishing until she talked through her block with me in a session. Giving voice to what she feared helped her to diminish that fear's weight enough to push it aside and keep writing.

Holding secrets in gives them power; bringing them out into the light can reveal their cracks. Never underestimate the value of sharing your burden with a trusted listener.

STOP ROMANTICIZING

On the other hand, there's such a thing as talking too much about a problem rather than facing it head-on. Rav was a struggling novelist who was fond of having a drink or ten and getting into long, involved discussions with friends about what a hard time he had writing. He seemed to love the difficulty more than he loved to actually write. There's a whole mythos around writers and struggle that can seem much more romantic than buckling down and working hard, and it's easy to fall in love with your own pain and fancy yourself a Hemingway or a Faulkner. But romanticizing struggle is more about ego—your idea of yourself as a writer—than about the work itself.

Don't be seduced into the persona of a brooding, troubled writer whose struggles are evidence of your misunderstood brilliance. If you find yourself having the same conversations over and over about what's getting in the way of your writing, step back and notice what it is that you keep repeating. What pattern are you enacting that you could break? What recurring issue could you look at in a different way?

Think of the issue as a bad habit, like biting your nails or picking your nose in public, something mundane and unsexy. How can you turn this romance with your pain into an ordinary roadblock, address it, and move forward?

SELF-TALK

Self-talk is like breathing, an involuntary action we don't even notice. But often when people do focus attention on it, they're shocked to notice the harsh and even cruel criticism they're leveling at themselves every day.

Carry a notebook or use your electronic device of choice to record your self-talk. For a week, observe and write down or vocally record what you say to yourself. Notice if you're making judgments or being unnecessarily mean. Is this the voice of your Shadow? How are you allowing your Shadow to trickle into your day without even realizing it—even when it's not about writing?

If you don't like the way you're talking to yourself and are ready to change it, spend another week tracking your self-talk and each time you record something, also record an opposite statement. For example, if you break a dish and you write down the thought, "I shouldn't have tried to carry so much at once—I'm always rushing and then end up losing time. I'm so stupid!" you might write after that, "I'm conscientious around the house and I make wise choices."

Try addressing yourself in the second or third person, as "you" or with your name. A study by psychologist Ethan Kross of the University of Michigan revealed evidence that making this minor linguistic shift can produce a significant change in the tenor of your self-talk. Addressing yourself like you would another person can help you react less emotionally and be more empathetic, as if you were talking to a friend.

See how it feels to record your initial statements and their opposites. Which kind of self-talk feels productive and puts you in an emotional state to accomplish your goals? Ultimately, you may land on some happy medium between the two extremes.

KEEP AND TOSS

Break your Shadow down into a two-columned list: *Keep* and *Toss*. What aspects of your Shadow and/or its role in your life are helpful to you—what would you keep? What aspects are intrusive or harmful to you—what would you throw away? What does this list show you about your Shadow and the impact it has on you?

USING OPPOSITION

In the interview exercise, what did your Shadow identify as his or her exact opposite? What would the embodiment of your Shadow's total antithesis look like? Like we did in the Shapeshifter chapter, use the Snapshot exercise to create an iconic image of your Shadow's opposite in addition to your Shadow.

What are these two beings like when placed on a level playing field? Can the image of your Shadow's opposite help to balance your Shadow out? For example, if you're struggling to manage self-talk coming from your Shadow, you could make an effort to allow both the Shadow and Anti-Shadow to speak up. If you find your Shadow crops up at dark or difficult moments, try calling upon your Anti-Shadow in those moments as well. Everything that exists in nature has an opposite, and you may find your Anti-Shadow can take some of the sting out of your Shadow's deepest cuts.

ICONS

We are storytellers and story consumers, and we draw inspiration from our favorite stories—in our work and in the way we live our lives. One of my clients was working hard on shedding an old way of seeing herself, so I encouraged her to pull inspiration for a new image of herself from fiction. Knowing what a big reader she was, I figured she'd pick something literary, maybe from Jane Austen, or even a more recent character like Elphaba or Lisbeth Salander.

So I laughed out loud when she told me she'd chosen Lara Croft, the badass tomb raider from video games and films who could just as easily skewer you with a crossbow as knock your eye out with one of her enormous boobs, their size rumored to be the result of a typo in the original game's programming.

To my client, though, Lara Croft wasn't a mere sexy cartoon; she embodied the essence of feminine power. This character became a touchstone we could return to in our sessions when one of us wanted to invoke a vision of this client at her strongest. The image of herself as Lara Croft was a totem she could draw from when she was struggling to find confidence.

What iconic image would you choose for yourself? What character, image, or idea embodies who you see yourself as becoming?

In this character's story, how does he or she attack a Shadow? What tools, techniques, or tricks does your totem character use in battle against a force of opposition? How can you mine this story for tips you can apply to your own conflict with your Shadow?

This next exercise fleshes out one option, of the many just given, for how to take power away from your Shadow.

EXERCISE: BATTLING THE SHADOW

Using your updated Character Sheet and the Shadow you described in the previous exercise, we're going to write their meeting, in screenplay format.

Create a slugline for the setting of this confrontation. For example,

EXT. WORLD WAR TWO BATTLEFIELD – DAY

INT. FOOD COURT AT A SHOPPING MALL IN HACKENSACK, NEW JERSEY – NIGHT

In a few sentences of action description, sketch out the setting where you and your Shadow will go head-to-head. It could be a setting taken from a work of fiction that inspires you, an actual place you've seen or heard about, a made-up setting you create—you decide. In just a few lines, give us a sense of where we are and what's happening.

Now, write out a scene between these characters that uses both dialogue and action. The content is up to you, but the scene must answer the following questions:

- How will you use your greatest strength(s) against the Shadow?

- What is your Shadow's greatest strength? How can you take it away from him/her?

- What is one secret you get your Shadow to reveal?

- What is one weakness your Shadow exposes for the first time?

- What do you decide to do with your Shadow at the end?

the hero is you

When you've completed the scene, read it aloud (enlist a trusted partner to read with you, if you like). Observe what it feels like to play both roles—to embody your Shadow and yourself as Hero.

What has shifted in your perceptions of your Shadow since the chapter began? In your perceptions of yourself?

Shadows on the Page

After many years in a high-powered corporate career, my client Beth had quit her job to focus full-time on writing for teens. Beth reminded me of Tina Fey, with her self-deprecating humor and wry delivery. She was also like Fey in her drive and ambition, but she could push herself too hard. Even after stepping off the corporate ladder, she hadn't lost any of the perfectionism or ambition that had made her so successful—and ultimately so burnt out—in her career.

When we began our work together, Beth had just started writing a novel, pushing toward the deadline associated with submitting her first draft to apply for a grant. Everything went smoothly until about a month before the deadline, when Beth's writing ground to an abrupt halt. She was only a few chapters away from the end, but she confessed that she was terrified of finishing the piece and discovering that it was terrible, that she was a fraud who had no business writing in the first place.

The real-life Tina Fey has spoken about this "imposter syndrome" and has advised others who struggle with it to "try to ride the egomania when it comes and enjoy it, and then slide through the idea of fraud." But Beth wasn't sliding. After making it her business never to "fail" in her corporate career by constantly overachieving, she had come to believe that, with enough elbow grease, she could power through anything. Now she was realizing that she could write and revise until her arms fell off and *still* not be good enough. The idea of failing at something she was working so hard at was paralyzing.

Faced with the risk of missing her deadline—an unpardonable sin, in Beth's worldview—she opened up to me for the first time about this fear of failure, which she'd always avoided discussing in the past. She talked about her corporate career: the stress of living in constant terror, always scrambling to stay two steps ahead of herself. She talked about how now, if she went more than a day without writing, she would start to panic and doubt whether she'd be able to write again the next time she sat down at her desk.

I knew it was hard for Beth to have this conversation. But when she acknowledged her fear as just another element of her life, instead of harboring it guiltily in a dark and hidden corner of her psyche, the terror lost some of its punch. When she recognized the toll the fear was taking on her, she saw its folly and released some of its power over her. Returning to her manuscript after our conversation, she didn't find it easy to jump back in, but reframing how she saw her roadblock made all the difference in finding her way past it.

Two weeks before Beth's application was due, she told me that as soon as she'd gone back to her novel, she'd had a shocking discovery.

"This is going to sound crazy," she began, "but I finally realized what's been bugging me about my manuscript all this time: the protagonist is the wrong gender."

Beth explained that, without being aware of it, she'd been trying to write the most accessible, "failure-proof" manuscript possible, which had led her to choose a male protagonist. But the clash with her Shadow had brought her the clarity to see that the story she'd been writing all along was that of a girl.

"So," she went on, "I have two weeks to rewrite the entire novel with a totally different main character. No bigs."

Though she was jokey, it was clear the task ahead of her was daunting. Months before, she'd mapped out a detailed plan of how she would use each week until the deadline. In her schedule, these two weeks had been allocated for final polishing. Completely rewriting the novel was *not* part of the plan, and going off-plan always made Beth anxious. But she was remarkably calm and focused.

"I don't know if I can do this," she told me, "but I'm gonna try."

Beth spent the next two weeks working like mad. She put in fifteen-hour days at her computer, barely eating or sleeping. She rarely saw her children or her partner. She told me later that she'd begun to feel like she was actually losing her mind.

She made it to FedEx with her finished manuscript fifteen minutes before they closed on the day of her deadline.

When we next spoke, I could see the change in her. Not only had she faced the fear that was holding her back, but she'd also accomplished what had seemed like an impossible task. After rewriting her entire novel in two weeks—and ending up with a draft she was proud of—her old fear of "failure" seemed laughable, almost quaint. She'd gotten past framing her work in those terms for the time being, and that realization was even more satisfying than she'd imagined.

"Maybe I'll get the grant, maybe I won't," Beth told me. "I hope I do, but if I don't, that's okay. Then I'll be on to the next thing." Getting the grant, publishing the novel—these goals were, to a large extent, out of Beth's control, decisions in other people's hands. But what she'd just accomplished had been up to her and her alone—and she'd crushed it.

Without her battle with her own Shadow, she'd never have discovered an essential missing piece in her manuscript, or that she wasn't writing totally authentically. Thanks to that battle, she could approach her next project from that place of being true to herself.

Rewriting Our Identities

In the Hero's Journey, in order to defeat a Shadow figure, the Hero must let go of the ego, the way she sees herself. In many stories, the Hero's battle with the Shadow represents a struggle between an old sense of self that is comfortable but no longer viable and a new identity that's waiting to emerge.

Sometimes, the hardest part about breaking the patterns or habits that hold us back is letting go of who we were when we first began those behaviors and admitting that we've changed. It can hurt to give up our old senses of self. But this rebirth, this atonement or becoming "at one" with a new version of ourselves, is key to moving forward and evolving as writers and people.

As part of annual New Year celebrations, Jews observe Yom Kippur or the "Day of Atonement"—a day not only to ask forgiveness for the sins committed in the old year, but to create a bridge between who we were in the year past and who we wish to be in the year to come. Facing the Shadow can be a moment of atonement in your writing life—an invitation to step into a new self.

> *This rebirth, this atonement or becoming "at one" with a new version of ourselves, is key to moving forward and evolving as writers and people.*

When I was twenty, during my senior year of college, a play I'd written won a fellowship to be produced at the Cherry Lane Theatre, the oldest continuously running Off-Broadway theater in New York City—an unprecedented opportunity for a young writer, and I was the youngest they'd ever selected for this honor. It was a tremendous experience, and when it was over, it left me completely blocked. I felt like Wile E. Coyote running off a cliff and plunging into the void of postcollege, unemployed life with all the time in the world to write and absolutely zero ability to put words to the page. Everybody was telling me to revise the play and generate new work, but no matter what I tried—giving myself assignments and deadlines, promising people I'd submit work to them and then flaking out at the last minute—nothing worked. The well was completely dry.

The longer I was blocked, the more afraid I became, and the more fear stopped me from writing, in a vicious cycle. My whole life, people had been telling me I'd be a famous writer someday, and I felt certain that if I couldn't step up to the plate at this moment and get my playwriting career started, it would mean that everyone had been wrong about me my entire life—including myself.

Mitchell Hurwitz, creator of the television show *Arrested Development*, once said that "the fear of writing . . . comes from the idea of yourself as a writer, being afraid that if you have bad ideas, write something bad, you'll discover you're not who you thought you were." I was so afraid of not being a Writer-with-a-capital-W—the title that had defined me all through school—that I couldn't do a writer's primary task. Not writing made me feel vulnerable, rudderless, and like I'd lost my identity.

It took years for me to see that my Writer identity had become a Shadow of its own, and that if I was ever to write again, I'd have to focus on the work itself, rather than what it did or didn't say about me as a person. The only way I was able to return to writing was by pulling away from everything that had defined me—no more theater world, no more submitting to contests or grants or prizes, no more talking about my work.

When I let go of those trappings of being a Writer-with-a-capital-W, I discovered that what gave me the greatest satisfaction in my new life was helping other writers—as a coach, as well as through teaching and editing. I discovered that the insights I'd gained from struggling with my Shadow gave me empathy for other writers, whether I was encouraging my students to get over their writer's block, giving prison inmates tools to express themselves, or helping my coaching clients battle their own Shadows.

Ultimately, my experience with the Shadow's self-destructive powers led me to bridge past and present—to become "at one" with both the pain and its remedy—to create the book you hold in your hands.

So What Now?

How do you take everything you've learned about what your Shadow is, where it comes from, how it's affecting your life, how to face it, and what elements of it you want to keep and discard, and turn all that into meaningful action that will help you accomplish your goals?

If this were a live coaching session, I'd pose that question to you and I'm confident the answer would pop out of your mouth. But because we're not sitting across from each other having this conversation, here's an exercise to help you begin addressing this question and living your way to its answer yourself.

EXERCISE: LIVING IN ATONEMENT

Return to the Mid-Book Check-In.

Beside each goal, write your Shadow's opinion of the goal, in his or her voice.

Does this voice still hold power for you? Do you still believe what it says? With the work you have done to vanquish the Shadow, do you find it is, as Alice said in Wonderland, nothing but a pack of cards? Or does it still drum fear into your heart or pull tension tight in your gut?

For each statement you've written from your Shadow, first cross it out (I find a black Sharpie works best) and then write why that goal is important to you.

How does it feel to obliterate the words of your Shadow? What's it like to see in black and white why these goals are so essential to you, why you're working so hard to achieve them?

Looking at these goals, what do you realize you've already accomplished?

Now that you have subdued the Shadow, you're capable of so much more than you even imagined. So it's time to raise the bar of those goals, to make them worthy of the conquering Hero you've become.

Keeping in mind the reasons you've written why these goals are important to you, ask yourself: *How could I push this goal further? Really challenge myself? What would turn this goal into one worthy of the Hero I've become?*

Write out a revised version of each goal, or brand-new goals you now feel better equipped to accomplish.

Look at the difference between the old goals you made before confronting your Shadow and the new, upgraded version. What has changed? What has remained constant?

If this is how you've evolved over the course of this process so far, what might you be capable of six months from now? A year? Five years?

---

the hero is you

Make of Yourself a Light

Ultimately, you may face the Shadow more than once over the course of your writing life. Each time will be an opportunity to unlock new reserves of strength within yourself and to develop tools to help you grow. You may be surprised by the results.

If you're like Beth, you may discover that facing what you most fear opens up new directions in your work that you'd never considered before. If you're like Brian, having the courage to be vulnerable may turn out to be the secret to finding your strength. If you're like me, perhaps your struggle with the Shadow will lead you to what truly motivates and inspires you.

Facing your Shadow means finding ways to grow from pain, to turn self-sabotage into self-renewal, to cast off what isn't serving you, keep what is, and use it to strengthen your writing and your spirit. Forged in the fire of adversity, you can become a beautiful weapon against anything that threatens your work.

Forged in the fire of adversity, you can become a beautiful weapon against anything that threatens your work.

We all have the potential to discover our inner Lara Croft, the most fearless, trailblazing part of ourselves, both in our writing and in our lives. That bravest Hero within us can shine light on even the darkest and most hidden corners of our inner worlds.

The process of writing itself is a process of illumination. We hold the torches up to our own Shadows to light the way for others. And our great hope is that, with enough shared light, we will all be able to face our fear of the darkness.

the superhero

finish what you started and apply what you've learned to revision

The encounter with the Shadow changes the Hero. Facing the greatest source of terror in their world, and in their own psyches, marks a kind of death for Heroes in myth. Whether meeting the Shadow meant a literal brush with physical death or a more metaphorical death, like the death of innocence or of a certain worldview, the experience changes Heroes so much that they are no longer the same people afterward.

This reborn Hero has truly absorbed the wisdom of the Mentor, been strengthened by the love of the Goddess, and is empowered after emerging from the battle with the Shadow. This is Hero 2.0, a more evolved person, more in tune with the best that she or he is capable of, less focused on self and more dedicated to the cause, and blessed with perspective and the ability to see the big picture.

I call this reborn Hero the **Superhero**.

Time and time again, I've seen this same rebirth happen for writers. Whether we have broken through a difficult or painful period in the work, or have simply been driving hard for a long time, each obstacle we overcome empowers us and gives us more momentum to propel us forward with increasing confidence. This momentum drives us, eventually, to a tipping point—it's a bit different for every writer, but some have described it as "the moment when I begin to believe I actually can do this" or "when I stop writing out of terror and start writing out of excitement."

This moment might come once in the process of working on a particular project, or it can come again and again in each round of work; as we've discussed, the Hero's Journey of your writing process isn't linear. But however it comes and whatever it looks like, it's when the gears finally click into place—when everything we've learned along the way empowers us enough that we're no longer so afraid. We see the light at the end of the tunnel and discover a newfound conviction that we are going to finish this piece of work.

When we begin to feel this confidence, we redefine what it means to be a Hero and become a Superhero.

When we begin to feel this confidence, we redefine what it means to be a Hero and become a Superhero. And we can channel that energy to help us finish and revise our work.

EXERCISE: REDEFINING "HERO"

By this stage in your process, you've seen that being a Hero is about more than the definition we outlined in chapter one. Let's revisit that definition and update it.

As a Hero, you were a person on a quest for identity and wholeness.

As a Superhero, list three surprising things you've learned about yourself since the beginning of the book.

As a Hero, you were a person with the potential for evolution.

As a Superhero, list three ways in which you've experienced growth since chapter one.

As a Hero, you were a person who said yes to the adventure.

As a Superhero, list three more things you want to say yes to in your life now that you've seen where this adventure has taken you so far.

Being a Superhero doesn't mean your journey is over. You may have crested the hill, but sometimes the downhill slope is the most challenging part of the ride.

The gift of reaching the Superhero stage of the journey—when you've gained the confidence and the knowledge to carry you through to the end—is knowing how to use everything you've learned to help you in the critical later stages of the writing process.

Writing Your Ending

Some writers, by the time they approach the ending of a piece, have gained so much momentum that they achieve a crystalline clarity and slide seamlessly into home plate. They already feel like Superheroes. Others . . . not so much.

Playwright Sam Hunter didn't tend to leave works unfinished. It usually took him about two years from getting the idea for a play to mounting a production of it, and he always had a new project in the hopper. But when it came to his play *I Am Montana*, he just couldn't seem to finish it.

It was a complicated show, a road trip story full of dream sequences and setting changes, with several interwoven plotlines. Every time he picked it back up, he thought this would be the time he'd see it through to its conclusion. But he could never find the right ending.

He put it away and worked on other plays that he completed and saw produced. He graduated from NYU and went to the Iowa Writers' Workshop. He kept studying his craft and learning more about writing for the theater.

Every time he pulled *I Am Montana* out for another try, he still couldn't figure out the end.

When he found himself writing the fortieth different ending for the piece, Sam threw up his hands. He felt like he had, he told me, "created a machine that was buckling under its own weight."

Finally, he decided to give this complicated play the simplest ending he could think of: a monologue. He figured, as he put it, "I guess I can just have the character tell the audience what this play is about."

He felt like the decision was a cop-out. But he was desperate to finally let the play go.

I Am Montana became the play that launched Sam as a writer. It was produced in London and Chicago, and ultimately won him acceptance into the elite playwriting program at Juilliard.

What Sam saw as a cop-out turned out to be a distillation of what he'd learned in his studies: to get out of his own way. He'd been so dead set on coming up with a clever ending that encapsulated everything he'd poured into the play, but ultimately, his experience finally taught him that sometimes the simplest answer is the best answer.

If you have a piece you're struggling to finish, this next exercise may help you figure out what the issue is and, like Sam did, get out of your own way.

EXERCISE: DIVINING WHAT'S STOPPING YOU FROM FINISHING

If you're having a hard time completing your piece, this mindfulness-based exercise is designed to help. Read through the whole text of part one before you begin.

Part One

Block off twenty minutes and make sure that during that time, you are completely undisturbed—no people and no electronic notifications of any kind. Turn your phone off and leave it in another room.

Set a timer for ten minutes. (If you don't own a kitchen timer, alarm clock, watch, or some other kind of timer that is not your phone, please get one! It's useful not just for this exercise, but for timed writing.)

Sit in a comfortable position and breathe deeply. Let each breath stir the clutter in your mind and clear it away.

the hero is you

Let this question be the point of focus you return to:

What is standing in my way?

Don't try to think of answers—just feel the feeling of being in this question. As Rilke said, "Love the questions themselves, as if they were locked rooms or books written in a very foreign language. Don't search for the answers . . . Live the questions now."

When ten minutes are up, write in your journal—longhand, if at all possible, not electronically—for another ten minutes and see what emerges in answer to this question.

Part Two

If the meditation and journaling brought you some clarity around what's preventing you from writing the ending, summarize the issue as an "I-statement" (see below for examples).

Let's look at some possible I-statements, and for each one, the tool you've already developed that you might use to address the issue.

I'm trying to choose between a couple different possible endings, and I can't decide which one is best.

Diagnosis: When you're struggling with a decision like this, it can mean you have competing motivations—for example, your idea of how the piece "should" end may be in opposition to the ending you sense may be right. Or you might find your original idea for where the piece was going conflicts with what has emerged while working on it.

Tool: Mentor. Connecting with your inner wisdom can often give you clarity on what direction feels most natural for the piece. When you think about each option, notice what your body is feeling. Does one give you a knot in your stomach, while another makes your pulse kick into a higher gear? Pay attention to these physical cues that you can interpret as markers of what direction is most true to the piece.

I've run out of concentration and can't focus.

Diagnosis: Focus is a renewable, but limited, resource. It does run out, but it can always be replenished. When we have been intensely focused for an extended period of time, we can reach a point when it becomes more difficult to concentrate.

Tool: Threshold Guardians. Identify the source of your distraction. Is it one of the issues we already targeted—social input, an itch to accomplish tasks, daydreams, or unrealistic expectations? Or is it something else? Can you ignore, absorb, or acknowledge what's causing you to feel distracted and move past it? If not, could it be an indication of something deeper? Look at some of the other options listed here to see if one of them may be underlying your struggle to focus.

I can't see the piece clearly enough to know which direction to take it in.

Diagnosis: When you've spent a long time working on a piece, and gotten deeply absorbed in it, it can be easy to lose perspective.

Tool: Shapeshifter. Zoom out and look at your piece through the eyes of a stranger, your Opposite, or some other point of view. See if you can find a completely new way to engage with your piece—by reading it aloud, or in a different location, or in a new format. If you haven't done so already, try one or all of the following: changing the font and other formatting in the document, printing it out, turning it into a PDF. When you've been staring at the same words for a long time, it can help to see them looking different than their familiar form.

I'm feeling uninspired.

Diagnosis: Working on the same project for a long time can be like being in a long-term relationship. After the honeymoon period ends, when you're no longer being driven purely by the Herald of inspiration, you come to rely more on familiarity and routine. But routine can become a rut, and the systems you've created may eventually begin to feel stifling.

Tool: Trickster. As you approach the end of your piece, it may be time to break your own rules, push your boundaries, and challenge yourself to try possibilities you've never considered before. Ask yourself what would be the *worst* way to end the piece, and try writing that, just as an exercise. Write an ending with a ridiculous twist, a corny deus ex machina, or the classic groaner of "it was all a dream." Allow yourself to write a few fake endings that are just for fun. One may dislodge a dormant idea that unlocks the actual ending from your imagination.

I'm feeling burnt out.

Diagnosis: Have you been driving yourself too hard to charge through to the end of this draft? When you're in a continual state of stress for too long, you can get into what Daniel Goleman calls "frazzle," a state in which your nervous system is constantly flooded with cortisol and adrenaline, preventing you from focusing. Of course, stressing out about being frazzled just brings on more mental fry.

Tool: Goddess. Remember to follow the natural cycles of your body—which includes your brain—as well as your process. If your brain is fried, give it a rest, even if you're on a tight deadline. Continuing to force yourself to work isn't going to help, and it might make things worse. Block out a chunk of time—at least half an hour, but ideally, one to four hours—to do something that refreshes you, energizes you, and gives your mind the opportunity to hit the reset button. Try a relaxing activity that will occupy your body but allow your mind to be unencumbered; taking a walk (particularly in nature) is my favorite, but something else may work for you. Be willing to take a few days off from the project to give it, and you, some space for your brain to relax and new ideas to emerge.

I'm afraid to finish it.

Diagnosis: As we saw in the Shadow chapter, fear can stop us in our tracks and prevent us from writing. As we also saw, the willingness to be vulnerable in answering that fear can help us overcome it.

Tool: Shadow. Ask yourself exactly what you're afraid of: That once you finish, you'll have to revise? That writing the ending will mean calling the piece "complete," even though it doesn't live up to your expectations? That finishing will mean sharing your work with others? That when this piece is done, you'll lose your sense of purpose? It may be one, some, or none of these options, but whatever fear is preventing you from completing the piece, identifying it as specifically as possible will help you face it using the tools and skills you developed in the Shadow chapter.

Bonus tool: Allies. For any of these situations, don't forget to turn to your Allies for help. Talking through the issue with an Ally—by describing the story *or* using your friend as a sounding board for what's at the heart of your hesitation—can bring you the insights, perspective, and peace you may need to move forward.

Integrating the skills you've learned and applying them to new situations is what it means to be a Superhero.

A Mentor's Advice

If nothing in that last exercise resonated with what's stopping you from finishing, you might simply need a kick in the pants.

Adam Wade loved telling stories in front of an audience: their energy, their responsiveness, their laughter and silence. But often, when he performed at the Moth live storytelling shows, he'd wind up losing the crowd by the end. After five minutes of talking, he would reach a great natural ending point, but the time slot for Moth performers was seven minutes long. Those last two minutes, he told me, felt like "the air going out of a balloon." He'd had the crowd in the palm of his hands, and now they were slipping through his fingers.

One night, after the show, Adam was chatting with his fellow storytellers when he felt a hand on his shoulder. It belonged to Jim O'Grady, an experienced storyteller and journalist who'd reported for the *New York Times* and was then at WNYC, the public radio station of New York City. His name was well known in storytelling circles, and Adam saw him as a Mentor.

Jim had enjoyed Adam's story, he said, but he had some advice for Adam.

"You don't have to end where you think you need to," he told the younger performer. "Get off the fucking stage."

It can be hard to know when to end a piece, but if we listen to our inner wisdom, we can separate the real ending from vamping. And that inner Mentor can tell us, like O'Grady did, when it's time to get off the fucking stage.

Super Emotional

Coming to the end of a piece can carry a mix of emotions, especially if you've been working on it for a long time. The ending can bring anxiety about whether you'll be able to tie it all up; excitement about how good it will feel to achieve this accomplishment; even sadness about having to leave behind this world you've created. If the work you've been writing is particularly personal or emotionally resonant for you, reaching the end may be cathartic in a way that could feel joyful or mournful—or both. Like any other ending in life, it is also a beginning, and brings a combination of celebration and sorrow.

When author Amanda Stern reached the final paragraph of one of her novels, she burst into tears—not just because it was over, but because she had finally, after months of working on the book, realized what it was actually about.

The novel told the story of a twelve-year-old girl whose father is using her as a kind of prop in a psychological experiment. The final scene has him wrapping a length of measuring tape around his daughter's head to measure its circumference. In that moment, the daughter thinks, *I'll let you do this for as long as you want, as long as you're this close to me.* As she wrote the scene, Amanda recognized that the whole novel was about her desire to be seen by her own father. Her tears came from her suddenly perceiving that "the whole book has been about this . . . and now I'm walking away from it."

But ultimately, what we are up to here is bigger than a single piece of writing. It's about translating our lives to ourselves, using writing as a way to better understand ourselves and our world. "Writing helps me figure me out," Amanda told me.

What you're creating is bigger than any single story. You are building an edifice with a wider base, deeper foundation, and more solid structure than any one project could encompass. You're creating a more holistic, more conscious process that you can apply not only to this project, but to the one after that, and the one after that.

After Heroes in myth vanquish their Shadows, they are able to seize their reward. This often comes in the form of a priceless boon—a golden fleece, a magical salt-grinder, the cure for the illness that plagues their homeland. But this boon that seems so valuable often looks like a trinket compared with the true gifts the now-Superhero has gained on the journey: courage, strength, knowledge, wisdom.

In Maureen Murdock's words: "The heroine must not discard nor give up what she has learned throughout her heroic quest, but learn to view her hard-earned skills and successes not so much as the *goal* but one part of the entire journey."

As you near the end of this portion of your journey and prepare for the road back—revision—remember the value of everything you've learned about your process. The boon of the draft is a great reward, no question, but the structures you've created and vulnerabilities you've strengthened can carry you through revision and far beyond, into your next adventure.

Says Joseph Campbell, "The Hero himself is that which he had come to find." As good as it feels to put the period at the end of the final sentence of a big project, your greatest satisfaction may come not from finishing your project, but from discovering what a seasoned writer you are becoming—one who can not only complete a piece, but create, over time, a body of work.

> *The work of being a writer is never done. Hopefully, that's good news.*

As one of my clients once said, "I'm going to finish this even if it takes a decade. Actually, it's not going to take a decade; it's going to take a lifetime." The work of being a writer is never done. Hopefully, that's good news.

Party Time

Reaching the end of your piece, no matter how you feel about doing so, is a cause for celebration. Many writers are so focused on what comes next that they forget to celebrate moments of accomplishment, or perhaps they feel it's too self-indulgent. But reaching a big milestone deserves special ceremony.

Ritual has always played a key role in societies, from ancient ceremonies to singing "Happy Birthday." Joseph Campbell calls ritual "the enactment of a myth"—in a sense, a way of acting out the psychological experience of the Hero's Journey and other mythic structures. These practices tell the story of who we are, comfort us with repetition, and distinguish this moment from all the other moments of our lives, marking it now and in memory as special and significant.

When you reach the end of your piece, don't gloss over the accomplishment. Call it out with a ritual-like celebration.

EXERCISE: CELEBRATING THE END

There are many different ways you can mark the milestone of completing your draft. Any of these can be undertaken solo or with an Ally or group of Allies. Choose the one or ones that resonate with you or come up with your own.

MAP: If you have continued to use the map from chapter one, decide what you would like to do to commemorate completing all its steps. You could frame it, set it on fire, emblazon it on a T-shirt. But whatever you do, recognize it as a symbol of all your hard work and how far it has taken you.

REWARD: What reward did you choose at the beginning for achieving your project goal? It's time to claim this boon, so hopefully you picked something wonderful! Enjoy your prize; share it with a friend or keep it all to yourself, whatever feels like the most juicy reward.

HERO PARTY: Invite some of your Allies to join you for a party that celebrates your accomplishment and inspires them on their own journeys.

CEREMONY: Create a ceremony to mark this milestone. You can model it on other ceremonies we use for rites of passage, or invent something wholly your own. Some possibilities:

- Have a ceremony that celebrates the birth of new life to acknowledge the "birth" of this completed project and confers blessings on the project and your dreams for its future.

- Throw yourself a graduation ceremony as you graduate from this stage of the process with pomp and circumstance.

- Hold a harvest festival to represent the end of your "Summer" of drafting and reaping the fruits of your labors.

- Make your ritual one of thanksgiving as you offer gratitude for everything you've learned and everything you have discovered you're capable of.

However you choose to mark the occasion, don't let the moment pass you by. The completion of a draft deserves to be acknowledged as a rite of passage in the timeline of your life as a writer.

Return and Revision

The claiming of the boon marks the end of the Hero's sojourn into the heart of this magical world and the beginning of the return journey. A mythical Hero, still far from home, must use all the skills and knowledge obtained on the journey to survive the perils of this trip. Known as "the Return" or "the Road Back," this can be the most perilous and fraught part of the adventure. Heroes may encounter the same or even more terrifying challenges and obstacles as before; a Shadow believed to be dead can reemerge more powerful than ever; and ultimately, the Hero must prove that he or she is truly a Superhero—capable of applying all the lessons of the journey—or the whole adventure has been for naught.

Some writers feel just that way about revision: that it's the most challenging part of the process. The stakes feel higher; the spontaneous and creative phase of drafting, in which there were no bad ideas, is over, and now it's time to get serious about what will make this piece truly the best it can be. For these writers, unhelpful habits, neuroses, and fears can rise to the surface during revision.

Others love revising. These writers consider drafting the agonizing part, full of those daunting blank pages with a blinking cursor at the top. The comfort of having something concrete to work with makes revising feel much more comfortable than pressure to create something out of nothing.

For many, it's a mix of both. Novelist Stefanie Pintoff told me she sees revision as an "analytical jigsaw puzzle," and she gets stuck when she's trying to fit a piece in that doesn't belong—inevitably, some element of the story she's attached to. Though it's painful, she reminds herself that she can always save it for the next book. Stefanie told me about one of her favorite characters, an FBI agent in a thriller series she was working on. She tried to work his backstory into each book in the series, but every time, when she stepped back and looked at the plot holistically, she recognized that his arc wasn't quite germane enough to the main plot. No matter how many great ideas she had about how to make him a bigger part of the story, she has had to keep saving him to focus on in a future book in the series.

The skills Stefanie has developed by working through the process on multiple novels—making sacrifices, following her inner wisdom, and changing perspective—continue to help her craft a revision that honors her story, even if it means holding her favorite character in reserve for next time.

Beginning the Return

No matter how you feel about revision, the first step is to take some time away from your work between when you finish the draft and when you begin to revise. As in the "Winter" we discussed in the Goddess chapter, this is a time of dormancy, letting ideas germinate under the surface, storing up the energy you will need to reapproach your work. It's also a chance to give your eyes a rest from the words you've written, so you can return to the work with more objectivity, seeing it more like a stranger as in the Shapeshifter chapter. Let the inner wisdom of the Mentor tell you how long this break should be—some writers don't take long, but others need to feel they have forgotten what they wrote so they can come back to it with truly fresh eyes.

Even if you're working on deadline, it's best not to rush. As a Superhero, you have the power to give yourself the gift of time—to recognize when the work needs longer to marinate and when it's ready to have your hands on it again.

When you dive in, you find yourself on a new voyage of discovery. But on this return trip, rather than taking each step into thin air and seeing the ground solidify under your foot, you're hacking a path through the dense wilderness of your draft, doing your best to identify where the road should go, what brush should be cleared away, and what flowers and trees need to be preserved.

When you dive in again, you find yourself on a new voyage of discovery.

Look back at what you discovered about your best ways of working in the Goddess chapter. What times of day are you most energized for writing? What kind of schedule do you find most effective? How much structure do you need to get your best work done, and what kind of structure? What motivates you? Most importantly, do all those discoveries remain true for revision? Or do you need to reevaluate your ways of working and adjust them to fit this different part of the journey?

There's only one way to find out: by doing. As you embrace your identity as the Superhero, employ all the tools of the past and be open to discovering new ones along the way.

Playing on Paper

Dancer/choreographer Kara Tatelbaum had spent two years working on a memoir about her dramatic rise and precipitous fall in the modern dance world and her experiences as a Pilates instructor in New York City. When she asked for my help, she had already revised the manuscript multiple times on her own. But when she'd sent it out to literary agents, she'd gotten a slew of rejections. The few agents who'd given specific feedback had said there wasn't enough of an arc or story. Kara was determined to hammer out that arc, to find that story. She didn't know how to do it on her own, though—she needed a fresh pair of eyes and some new ideas about how to work. So we rode the Metro-North train up the Hudson Valley to her parents' home by the river and spent a weekend tearing the manuscript apart.

Kara had made an outline that we tried to use to organize the revisions required, but that quickly became confusing and hard to follow. I suggested we do something she'd never done before: lay out the entire manuscript, chapter by chapter, on the floor of the bedroom. The carpet of papers went wall-to-wall.

Most of us have become so accustomed to working in the digital space that it's easy to forget how helpful it can be to get tactile. Doing so allowed us to treat the document like a puzzle we could solve if we got all the pieces in the right order.

We moved two chapters from the middle to the beginning. We grouped several chapters together that had been spread out. We cut some moments and added placeholders for others that were missing from the narrative. One chapter at a time, we molded the memoir until it had a more substantive plot arc. By the time the setting sun lit up the surface of the Hudson, this series of episodes had become a story—Kara's story.

Anne Lamott shares a similar anecdote in *Bird by Bird* about revising her second novel. The revision she emerged with from that process was not the definitive version; her editor rejected it, and she went on to start over, essentially from scratch, by writing a forty-page plot treatment that ultimately became the book. Likewise, Kara did not come out of our weekend with her memoir done or ready to share it with the world. She had to write a handful of new chapters, rewrite several of the existing chapters, and then revise the whole manuscript again so it would all feel consistent.

When, after all that work, an agent did offer to represent the memoir, the revision process started anew with the agent's feedback. Drafting only happens once, but revision can happen over and over and over again, until you feel as if you've lived in this tunnel forever. You can't remember what life was like before you started revising, and you can't imagine what it will be like to ever complete the work.

But one of the Superhero's powers is the ability to zoom up, up, and away and view the bigger picture. From that vantage point, you can see all that you've accomplished and the way that everything you've done—

even the tasks that seemed futile at the time, or feel futile now—served the piece and got you further toward a final draft.

Revising Perspective

Each round of revisions teaches you a lesson about writing and about yourself. The trick is having the Superhero's supersonic hearing to be attuned to those lessons.

Negin Farsad's memoir was supposed to be funny; it was called *How to Make White People Laugh*, after all. She'd written TV shows, plays, movie scripts—all comedies—and did stand-up, not to mention masterminding a comic poster campaign for the New York City subway system to fight bigotry with "delightful" comedic messages about Muslims.

When it came time to write a chapter about one of the most horrible moments of her life, though, she wasn't sure how to make it funny. And in the first draft, she didn't.

The chapter told the story of being seventeen years old and appearing in a play at her Palm Springs high school, a comedy in which she'd been part of a love triangle. The theater club was performing their show for an audience of three hundred boys who were usually in P.E. and auto shop during that period. At the moment in the play when the leading man chose zaftig, bespectacled Negin over the skinny blond—per the script—the audience exploded with expletives and insults, hurled at Negin. She told me, "It was the most crushing and humiliating day of my teen life."

Negin hadn't intended to include such a raw scene in her memoir; she'd planned to "hide all my feelings behind a layer of comedy." But she surprised herself by digging deep and letting herself say what she felt. It was naked, painful—true to life, but hard to read.

When she returned to it in revision, though, she was able to layer humor into it. Rather than hiding behind the comedy, she looked back at this moment from years ago and genuinely saw the funny.

And she realized that, in this past moment of utter humiliation, she'd also been incredibly strong—stronger than she'd ever given herself credit for.

That day, "I was a mess," she told me, "but I finished the play and then performed it again the next day and then became a comedian." She said the event lit a fire under her and motivated her—not just *I'll show you* but "I will keep showing you three hundred kids over and over again for the rest of my life."

Writing about the moment brought it back for her, in all its ugliness; revising showed her what that event ultimately meant in the story of her life. The worst day of her teen life had turned into the catalyst for the danger-defying, boundary-breaking comedy that became her mission as an artist and as a person.

When we revise our work—crystallizing it, excavating its meaning, jettisoning the extraneous, and clarifying its inherent truth—we are giving ourselves the opportunity to do the same with our ways of seeing ourselves and the world. To be the Superhero is to also revise our lives.

the steed

share your work — and yourself — with the world

In myth, when Heroes have survived their return travels, they cross a final threshold, leaving the magical world and returning to their own, where they reconnect with their community. In many ways, this can be the most difficult part of the Hero's Journey: trying to explain to the people who've stayed safely at home all this time what it was like battling monsters in fantastical landscapes.

Likewise, as a writer, you know all the battles you've fought to produce this project, but the people reading or watching it for the first time can't see that. All they see is the finished product. What looked so good on the page and sounded so brilliant read aloud to yourself in the privacy of your home can take on a totally different shape in the unforgiving light of public view.

But sharing your work is also a special—and important—test of your heroic abilities and a crucial step in your journey. We can all write for the audience of the desk drawer, but by inviting our audience to be collaborators in the process, we truly bring the work to its full potential, and discover how we're capable of growing as writers and humans through the experience.

An Insulating Horse

In *The Hero with a Thousand Faces*, Joseph Campbell retells the Irish legend of the hero Oisin. After traveling to the magical Land of Youth and marrying its princess, Oisin wishes to return to his home in Ireland to visit his family. Reluctantly, Oisin's fairy wife gives him a white horse that she promises will carry him wherever he wants to go. But she warns her husband, "If you come down from the steed or touch the soil of Erin with your foot, the steed will come back that minute, and you'll be where he left you, a poor old man."

No problem, thinks Oisin, but you can probably guess what happens. During his trip, he ends up accidentally touching the green ground of Ireland, and he loses not only his steed, but his whole magical life, including his princess wife.

This "insulating horse"—a tool that stands between the Hero and the earth while still allowing him to visit the ordinary world—is a common theme in folktales from all around the globe. Many ancient cultures in places from Uganda to Persia to Mexico believed that the power possessed by sacred individuals, such as divinely appointed rulers, was like electricity—it could be sucked away if the person came into contact with a good conductor. In Oisin's case, those rolling emerald hills of his homeland proved too strong a conductor for his power and sucked the magic right out of him. Had he managed to stay on his steed, though, he'd have been able to contain it.

In other words, if Oisin was a copper wire teeming with electricity, the horse was the rubber grounding his current. Remove the buffer, and the current surges out.

Campbell makes the point that in every arena of society, we use symbols to insulate ourselves, from the deliberate ways we choose to dress to the complicated rules of etiquette. Sporting business attire at an office can send the message "I belong here" and insulate the wearer from appearing to be an outsider. Standing alone in public waiting for a friend to arrive, tapping away at our phones insulates us from unsolicited interaction with strangers. An unmarried friend of mine wears a zirconium "engagement" ring when she travels to insulate her from unwanted advances (though this can backfire since even a ring doesn't dissuade the most determined and least appealing suitors).

These insulating symbols protect those who wield them; like Oisin's steed, they allow their carriers to retain their powers, to repel undesired encroachment from the world. To retain your confidence and vision for your project, you will need to develop your inner **Steed** to carry you through the rocky landscape of other people's opinions.

Whether you've ever ridden a horse or only seen them on a screen, you know that they elevate their riders, but just slightly. When you're on horseback, you can still see and hear everything that's happening on the ground, but you have a little bit of distance from the earth. The Steed's job is to help you find this balance—to elevate you enough to protect you from unhelpful feedback, but keep your eyes and ears open to what is useful. Horses also lend their riders power, protection, and strength—there's a reason knights rode them into battle. A healthy dose of perspective can do the same for you.

To retain your confidence and vision for your project, you will need to develop your inner Steed to carry you through the rocky landscape of other people's opinions.

A Steed leaves you open to the elements. On a Steed, you can ride through critique and criticism, hearing everything that's said, and take it in with an open, but not unprotected, heart. You can choose what to accept and reject.

A horse provides more than just transportation—it is also a companion. A key element of finding this place of perspective within yourself is giving yourself compassion, treating yourself kindly and without judgment, the way our animal companions treat us (with the possible exception of cats).

But before any of this happens, you must determine when your work is ready to share.

Jan was attending her first writers' conference and decided to splurge on a critique on her novel from a literary agent. She was a little anxious about sharing her rough draft with a publishing industry professional, but figured it was too good an opportunity to pass up.

The agent tore the manuscript to shreds. Jan disagreed strongly with most of the feedback, but also knew this agent was a professional—she'd trusted her to be constructive. Cowed, confused, and downhearted, Jan put the project in a drawer and didn't write for the next two years.

When she became my client and began writing again, Jan acknowledged that while the encounter had been traumatic, she'd learned a valuable lesson about sharing her work too early. During our work together, the same annual conference was coming up, and after some consideration, Jan decided her new manuscript wasn't ready for outside feedback yet. This novel was different from anything she'd written in the past, and she wanted to do everything she could to make it the best it could be before showing it to anyone with the power to impact her.

Even gentle, thoughtful critique can feel abrasive if the work isn't ready to be exposed to another person's opinion. This is why it's crucial to have trusted Allies. A good Ally can tell you when you seem ready to expose the work to critique. When that time comes, an Ally can give you constructive comments that will contribute to the piece and further your development as a writer.

> *Accepting feedback, like any other aspect of the writing process, is a skill to be honed.*

Accepting feedback, like any other aspect of the writing process, is a skill to be honed. Whether your tendency is to take it too personally, to follow it to the letter, or to dismiss it too readily, many of us struggle when it comes to knowing exactly how to absorb the input of others. If you find this difficult, try the following exercise next time you're about to receive feedback.

EXERCISE: PREPARING FOR FEEDBACK

Use this exercise to bookend your next experience of feedback. Do part one shortly before you share your project for the first time with a writing partner, critique group, or other Ally or Allies. Set aside time to do it the day before or even the same day that you know you'll be getting feedback.

Part One

SETTING INTENTIONS: Answer the following questions.

- Are you looking for larger-scale input (i.e., "what should happen in this story?") or smaller-scale (i.e., "what do you think about the characters' relationship in this scene?")?

- What is the tenor of the feedback you'd find most useful right now: tough love, supportive validation, ruthless honesty, gentle observations, encouragement to continue?

- Is there some specific issue you're hoping the feedback will illuminate? If so, what?

- What do you consider your blind spot, the aspect of your own work you find most difficult to evaluate?

- If you could wave a magic wand to fix the aspect of your piece you're struggling with most, what would change in your current pages?

With your answers to those questions in mind, summarize in a few sentences what you hope to achieve by getting input on your work.

ASKING FOR HELP: List two or more aspects of the project you think need the most work that you want to ask your Ally/Allies for help with.

ESTABLISHING GROUND RULES: List what you *will* and *will not* do in this feedback session. A few examples:

I will . . .	I will not . . .
Remember that (so-and-so) likes to be very directive	Verbally defend my choices
Keep an open mind	Change my piece to fit someone else's vision for it

PROJECT VISION: Restate your vision for the project to remind yourself of what you're trying to do and to use as a rubric for selecting which feedback to apply.

STEED: Complete these sentences:

- I need my Steed to insulate me from . . .

- I need my Steed to leave me open to . . .

Notice how your experience of getting feedback changes when you have clarified your intentions, expectations, and vision beforehand.

Part Two

Complete this section of the exercise after you've gotten the feedback—ideally, the same day.

How did you feel at the end of the feedback session?

HOPES: Look back at part one to see what you hoped to achieve by getting input on your work. Do you feel like this was accomplished?

HELP: Did you ask for the help you needed? If so, did you get it?

GROUND RULES: Did you struggle to follow any of the rules you set out? Which, if any, do you want to work on next time?

Complete the following sentences:

- Next time, I want to work on listening to . . .

- Next time, I want to work on protecting myself from . . .

Paying attention to what worked for you and what frustrated or challenged you will help you continue to receive feedback with intention and self-awareness and make it as useful as possible.

———————

Leaving Your Saddlebags at the Door

Loretta was extremely fearful of other writers' opinions. She'd been in a critique group from which she'd departed somewhat acrimoniously after a defensive blowup at the other members, and since then, had been afraid to share her work with anyone. She hated the idea of being judged and was reluctant to trust other writers, even though there was an active and social writing community in her town.

I challenged her to face this fear head-on. Over the course of our work together, as we talked about her default reaction of defensiveness, she peeled away old layers of hurt and discovered that she could trace her reluctance to trust others back to a childhood fear of abandonment. Separating her past experiences from her current writing life helped, and so did admitting she had a tendency to push people away preemptively.

I cheered for Loretta when, after years of isolation, she decided to not only join a new writers' group, but also become the coordinator of groups for a local writers' organization. She'd be in a group herself *and* she'd be helping connect other writers with partners. She'd jettisoned, or at least reduced, her outdated defense systems and found the confidence to let other writers help her—and, in doing so, recognized that she could help them, too.

When we sit in a room full of writers, each member of the group brings a saddlebag of conditioning and pain along. Our job as members of a community, and as Heroes, is to be conscious of our old injuries and keep them separate from the conversation. Be aware of your own tendencies when it comes to responding to feedback: do you get defensive, apologize, feel the need to explain? Ask yourself where those impulses come from and how you can leave them at the door.

Knowing the history of your old hurts may help remind you that everyone whose work you're evaluating has scars and soft spots of their own. Being a good Ally to your fellow writers means finding the right balance between honoring these wounds with kind, constructive language without holding back the honesty your Allies count on getting from you.

Taking the Good with the Bad

When you gather input on your work—from a writing partner, a workshop group, a trusted Mentor, or whomever you select—you must also choose what advice to take and what to let go. Most likely, you've gotten some compliments as well as some constructive criticism, but most of us have a tendency to focus more on the negative feedback than the positive. Numerous psychology studies have proven that it's human nature to do this. Some scientists say this goes back to our prehistoric ancestors—the early humans who were most attuned to negative events (like, say, remembering where the saber-toothed tiger attacked last time) would've had the strongest chance of survival. Luckily, getting impaled on a massive incisor isn't a major concern for most of us anymore, so we can allow ourselves to hear it all—the praise and the problems.

As you evaluate what advice to apply and what to cast aside, tap into the deeply rooted Mentor within you who knows what's truly best for your own work.

EXERCISE: MOVING THE NEEDLE

This exercise is designed to help you choose which feedback to discard and which to incorporate into your work.

Begin by laying out all the comments in front of you in an orderly way that makes sense to you, is clear and easy to read, and is completely democratic, giving no precedence to any particular piece of advice. You may find it helpful to transfer any notes you've received to a new document that wipes them of the identity of whoever gave them to you. You could type them up or handwrite them in a list, put them on notecards or Post-Its, or plug them into a spreadsheet—whatever resonates with you.

Make sure to include positive comments as well as criticism. If you didn't write compliments down while receiving the feedback, try to remember them and write them down.

Take a moment to connect with your inner Mentor in whatever way resonates with you. You might want to revisit the poem you wrote in the

Mentor chapter, remember a past moment of following your gut, or sit quietly and breathe for a few minutes.

Take a look at the positive comments. Read each one without rushing through them and really take in what the person has said about your work. When you've finished that, read through the rest of the critiques.

Now imagine you have a dial like the ones you see attached to blood pressure cuffs, or on the dashboard of your car to show speed and how hard the engine is working. This dial looks like this:

This dial is connected to your inner Mentor.

Read a piece of feedback and notice how your Mentor responds. If you get a "blah" feeling, that's a NO. If you feel resistant but can't bring yourself to dismiss the advice entirely, it's a MAYBE. If you feel a strong resonance, excitement, or curiosity, the needle pushes into YES.

Use this dial to measure your response to different kinds of feedback. Make sure not to rush—sometimes, initial resistance can simply mean the work required would be daunting, but it might be just what you need.

After you've tested out every piece of feedback, look over the NOs again and make sure you definitely don't want to do any of them. Then discard them. It might feel good to literally throw them away.

Now focus on the MAYBEs. Remember your Steed and notice: Are you insulating yourself from painful but helpful truths? Or are you protecting yourself from advice that, while you can see value in it, doesn't serve your vision for the piece?

Applying this to the feedback you receive can help you determine what to use and what to discard.

———————————

Carrots to Potatoes

The cycle of soliciting feedback and revising can happen many times at this stage of your journey, until eventually, you reach a stopping point.

Writers often ask me how to know when they're finished. One of my colleagues at Penguin was editing a debut novel that had gone through many rounds of revision. She sent the author a final line edit of very light notes, changing a word here, a sentence there, and expected it to be a fast and simple turnaround.

So she was surprised when the manuscript came back with dozens of tiny adjustments made by the author—changes my colleague hadn't asked for. In one scene, the protagonist was helping her mother prepare dinner by chopping carrots. The author, for no apparent reason, had changed the carrots to potatoes. She had become so accustomed to making extensive changes in each round of revision that the minimal markup had made her feel—whether consciously or subconsciously—that she had to find more things wrong with the manuscript. But she wasn't making the book better at that point; she was just needlessly rearranging it.

When you find yourself changing carrots to potatoes, you're done. Resist making edits that are arbitrary, unnecessary, or just plain silly. Recognize that, no matter how much you may be afraid of the next step, you've done all you can do. If you are worried that it's not perfect, rest assured: it never will be. But at a certain point you have to allow it to be, in playwright Sam Hunter's words, "a snapshot of your writing" at this particular moment in your career.

Your work is ready to share with the world.

Know Your Motivations

A Steed becomes even more crucial when we have drafted, revised, and revised again, and are finally ready to share our work with people who may make decisions about its future. Because even though these decisions have little or nothing to do with your value as a person, it can be very difficult not to internalize them on a deeply personal level.

That's why it's vital that, before you send your work out, you check in with yourself and clarify exactly what you want for this project, and why.

Nohealani had just started writing picture books for children, but everybody in her writers' group—most of whom had been writing for longer—was submitting manuscripts to publishers. She figured she'd better do the same, and sent out the first story she'd written. After a slew of form rejection letters, she got one personal note from an editor telling her that her writing showed promise but she had a lot more to learn about the craft, and pointing out specific examples of rookie mistakes she'd made. Nohealani felt humiliated. She'd been trying to do what she thought she was supposed to, and it had yielded rejection and failure.

But she took the editor's advice to heart. She read hundreds of published books, took a writing class, and wrote several more manuscripts that she *didn't* send to anyone. The more she studied, the more embarrassed she was that she'd sent that very first manuscript to publishers. By the time she was ready to submit her work again, she was a seasoned student of picture book writing as a science and an art, and she knew more about the marketplace. She'd even made a careful study of different editors' books, so she'd know whose taste made them most likely to be drawn to her work. She felt much more confident, and knew that the next rejection letter she got wouldn't skewer her for any newbie errors.

Sharing your work is a conscious act that connects you with your original vision for the project and your mission as a writer. Before you start sending out anything you've written, take a moment to check in with yourself about why you want to share your work and what you hope to get out of the experience.

EXERCISE: CREATING A STEED

When you are considering submitting your work on any professional level—to a literary agent, publisher, contest, grant application, festival, production company, award committee, graduate program—try this exercise beforehand. Its purpose is to help you clarify your motivations, perform a brief emotional check-in, and give you a touchstone to return to once your work is out there in the world.

Take a few moments to connect with the piece of writing in question. If it's brief, you might want to reread it; if it's long, you may prefer to skim it or flip through it. You might just want to sit with the printed-out pages in your lap so you can feel the weight of what you've created.

Now answer the following questions:

- What initially inspired me to write this piece?

- What is my greatest dream for this project? What impact do I hope it will have?

- What do I hope to feel by having that dream realized?

- What else in my life gives me the same or similar feelings?

- What moments in this process have given me the most joy?

- What is the worst thing that could happen with this project?

- How would that feel?

- What past experiences made me feel similarly? How did I overcome them?

- Restate your vision for the project. How does sharing the project in this way serve this vision?

- Restate your mission as a writer. How does sharing your work in this way serve your mission?

When you are done, take a moment to read over everything you've written and see what particularly resonates.

Trace the outline of a horse onto a piece of paper, or create it digitally. Pull the answers that meant the most to you and write them inside the horse. Create your own Steed, filled in with your feelings about this project.

You could post this Steed in your writing area or stash it somewhere to pull out when you need a reminder of the foundations that underlie your work, no matter what happens to it out there in the world.

Validation

So you've written, revised, gotten feedback, revised again, gotten more feedback, polished the piece to a high gloss, done your research about where to send it, and sent it off. And now you wait . . . and wait . . . and wait.

I've seen many writers get into an excited frenzy as they prepare to submit their work and send it off, only to have their balloons slowly deflate as the days and weeks and even months tick by with no response.

Sharing your work with professionals can give you a deadline and a goal, provide a motivation to make the piece the best it can be, and raise the stakes of what you're doing. It takes your writing out of its bubble and into the great wide world, where so much more is possible. It might even, ultimately, bring you the recognition you're seeking.

But if you're sending your work out in search of the happy rush of external validation, you might want to find another way to get it—or consider what exactly you're hoping to hear. The only source of validation you can consistently rely upon is within you.

This holds true for all types of artists—not just writers. In the world of classical music performance, positions with orchestras are highly coveted and fought for intensely. Very few musicians are able to build entire careers as soloists or in small ensembles without having put in time with an orchestra first, and symphonies provide the only opportunities for consistent work, livable income, health insurance, and other key benefits in this shrinking and extremely competitive field.

After years of study, Jonah, a classical violist, got on the audition circuit. He sent demo recordings and attended auditions in cities all across the United States. Sometimes, he was called back; other times, he didn't even get close. He almost never got any feedback letting him know why he hadn't won the job, what he could've done differently, what the selection committee had preferred about the candidate they chose. He was pouring everything he had into these auditions, and all he got back was silence.

At first, Jonah took each loss personally. He felt he had something to prove, and each time he didn't accomplish his goal, he berated himself about his "failure," agonized over what he'd done wrong, and wondered if he ought to give up entirely.

Meanwhile, though he hadn't yet secured a symphony position, his talent and skill were being acknowledged in other ways. Jonah won grants, was selected for elite summer music festivals, and got to tour the world with various ensembles. He even played at Carnegie Hall—multiple times.

After several years, Jonah began to see his process with a new perspective. "If I'm going to stay in this," Jonah told me he'd realized, "it can't be life and death every time, and I have to stop wondering if I'm good enough."

To succeed, Jonah ultimately had to let go of his desire for external recognition and find other ways to validate himself, like acknowledging himself for other kinds of successes, both external (Carnegie Hall—not too shabby) and internal (reaching a goal or achieving a certain sound during a practice session). As judge and jury for his own work—hearing himself every day, witnessing his own incremental improvements—his standards for himself were often as high as or even higher than the standards of his evaluators. As long as he kept his expectations at that level, his work would continue to be good; the trick would be finding a symphony that felt his particular sound was a good fit for what they needed.

He'd had enough successes to know that he was good. Now his greatest challenge was to simply keep going and not take the rejections personally.

External validation feels great, no question. But it's something we have no control over. We can always go to our Allies when we need a vote of confidence, but industry professionals—agents, editors, producers, and others—are not paid to make us feel good. Their job is to find the very best writing that's out there, that meets their company's needs, and sign it on with the hope that it will make money for their employers. Most are passionate about craft and deeply committed to making the work they acquire the best it can possibly be. But they say no to hundreds more people than they say yes to—because that's their job. When they say no, they're saying no to *this project*—not rejecting you or your value as a person or even as an artist.

At this writing, Jonah is still in the middle of this process. He still struggles with confidence in the face of rejection. But the Steed he has developed to bounce back from those moments of self-doubt has kept him going in the pursuit of his calling and the continual refinement of his craft.

We all crave acceptance and validation, but we can't always depend on those coming to us from the outside world. Sometimes, the world seems determined to invalidate the work we're doing. But even that can yield happy results in the long run.

In 2006, comedian Jessica Delfino was publicly denounced by the U.S. Catholic League for her comic song "My Pussy is Magic" after it went viral on YouTube. In a press release, Catholic League president William A. Donohue declared of the song, "At a time when radical Muslims are accusing Americans of harboring a depraved understanding of liberty, it only provides ammunition to the enemy."

No matter who's doing the decrying, it doesn't feel great to be decried; on the other hand, considering the Catholic League had also denounced such artists as painter Chris Ofili and comedian Sarah Silverman, Jessica was flattered to be in such famed company. Donohue was thoughtful enough to also include in his press release the locations and dates of Jessica's entire national tour—which promptly sold out. The publicity led to a record deal for her. Jessica sent Donohue postcards from every city on her tour.

Whether you're waiting for an accolade that never comes or hoping for bouquets of roses and getting tomatoes thrown at you instead, you'll find external validation to be a tricky and unpredictable beast. But the Steed you develop within yourself can help you stay the course and focus on what's most important: continuing to write.

Rejection

In 1991, journalist Anne Fadiman got a big break: she was commissioned to write a three-part piece for the *New Yorker*. Anne had never written for the *New Yorker* before, a Holy Grail gig in the journalism world, and she quit her job at *Life* and spent a year working on the massive article. She was just finishing up the piece, working from her bed during a difficult pregnancy, when she got the devastating news that Robert Gottlieb, the editor in chief of the *New Yorker* who'd commissioned the article, had been fired and replaced with Tina Brown.

"I felt as if a meteor had hit the earth—or at least *my* earth," Anne told me. Anne was certain Brown, known for her coverage of celebrity news, would have little interest in the piece Anne was writing about a Hmong child with epilepsy and the culture clash between her doctors and her family. Before exiting the magazine, Gottlieb paid Anne for the piece and reimbursed all her expenses, but Anne doubted it would be published. Still, she wouldn't know for certain until the *New Yorker* gave her a definitive answer, so she anxiously waited.

A full year after Gottlieb's departure, Anne finally received a letter from Brown, who misspelled both Anne's first and last names as she informed the writer that she was killing the story.

Rejection never feels good, no matter whom it comes from or how many times we've experienced it. Psychologist Guy Winch explains that the agonizing, almost physical pain of rejection may stem from evolutionary origins; in the days of our hunting and gathering ancestors, a social rejection from the group literally meant death, as the person being excluded would be unable to eat, mate, and stay safe from carnivorous beasts. According to Winch, brain scans have revealed that rejection and physical pain both activate the same regions of the brain—so much that test subjects who'd taken Tylenol before being put through a simulation of rejection reported less emotional pain than those who hadn't.

Winch also talks about how self-criticism can compound the pain of rejection. Having your work rejected or criticized can be just what a dormant Shadow needs to reemerge in your life and make you feel even

the hero is you

worse. The voice of the Shadow can turn a self-contained event into just one in a series of supposed "failures" it lambasts you for.

In addition to employing the tools you've already developed for combating the Shadow, use the Steed to give yourself perspective on how the rejection fits within the larger context of your work and your life. What can look like a slammed door today can turn out to be a gateway to a whole new direction you might not have otherwise considered.

After receiving Brown's letter, Anne was crushed but undaunted. She used her unpublished piece to secure a book contract and spent the next four years working on the manuscript. Published in 1997, *The Spirit Catches You and You Fall Down* went on to win the National Book Critics Circle Award for Nonfiction, the *Los Angeles Times* Book Prize, and the Salon Book Award. It was embraced by critics and launched Anne's career as an author.

Anne told me, "I now look back on that letter as one of the greatest gifts I have ever received, since without it, I never would have turned the story into a book, and my life would have been completely different."

Anne didn't have any control over the staff changes at the *New Yorker* or the editor's taste or interests. All she could control were her own actions in the face of the rejection. She chose to keep working, and to keep holding herself to her personal highest standard. She was bruised, but she got back on the horse and kept riding.

A Steed for Success

All Rebecca Serle had ever wanted was to be a writer. She moved to New York City in 2007, where she juggled freelance gigs and struggled to make her rent. She got a literary agent, but wasn't able to secure publication for the picture book manuscripts the agent had sent out. Her great dream, though, was to get the young adult novel she'd been working on published.

When Rebecca finally finished the novel and her agent sent it out to editors, her world was abruptly turned upside down. Editors scrambled to acquire the novel, and the winner offered Rebecca a huge advance for two books. Within weeks, a movie deal was in the works, and mere months later, a director was attached, stars were being considered, and Rebecca was reading a script of her novel by the screenwriter of the indie hit *(500) Days of Summer*.

Magazines and blogs profiled Rebecca, hailing her as a wunderkind. Before she knew it, the soft-spoken twenty-six-year old who was terrified of public speaking was walking down a fashion runway to promote her book, "taking meetings" in Hollywood, and managing a staff that included a literary agent, a film agent, a publicist, a manager, and more.

Rebecca's friends and family were thrilled for her, and kept saying things to her like, "Aren't you excited?" and "Isn't this amazing?" and, probing deeper, "Why don't you seem happier about all this?"

Of course, Rebecca was happy and excited. She was also stressed out and terrified. Her dreams had come true on a swift and epic scale, and with that came a major adjustment in perspective. She couldn't afford to be starry-eyed or naive. She had to become a savvy businesswoman, a tough-skinned industry professional, and a powerful self-advocate—overnight.

Without any precedent to follow, she needed to figure out her best methods for coping with situations she'd never dreamed of dealing with. What if she hated the movie? What if people online wrote nasty things about her and her book? And, most importantly, how could she continue writing, not only to fulfill that second book in her contract and beyond, but because, all the excitement and fanfare aside, she was a working writer doing a job she loved and wanted to continue doing well?

Rebecca struggled with a deep-seated fear that she was a fraud, that she'd somehow fooled everyone into believing she was a talented writer, but that soon they'd discover the truth. This old Shadow, revived by her successes, haunted her and made her doubt whether she deserved these accolades at all.

Success is not a magic happiness pill, and comes with its own inherent challenges. Positive attention can threaten your ability to look objectively at your work and yourself. Critical acclaim can revive old Shadows you'd thought were vanquished. Achieving external success can make you feel like you're losing control—it can seem like other people are making you, and they can break you, too.

But through all this, Rebecca discovered that her deepest satisfaction still came from the writing process itself, and that this process was also her greatest source of strength. Returning to the page, moving forward on her new project, and focusing on the work helped her quiet the voices of doubt.

Success is not a magic happiness pill, and comes with its own inherent challenges.

By continuing to write, Rebecca saw that, in her words, "there is no right way to do it; nobody is an expert; nobody is more or less deserving of how their career unfolds; and everyone has their own process." As she figured this out on the page, she and her writing grew stronger.

Since 2012, when Rebecca's debut novel *When You Were Mine* came out, she has gone on to publish several more young adult novels and become the cocreator of a television series based on her *Famous in Love* trilogy. She went from taking meetings in Hollywood to running them. Her life looks completely different now than when she was the new girl in town wondering if she'd ever get published. But what has remained constant is her commitment to her craft.

Writing became her Steed. It grounded her, gave her perspective, stopped her from believing her own hype, and offered her a wellspring of confidence that was deeper and more lasting than the quickie buzz of external validation. It kept her focused on what her real dream had been all along: to be a working writer.

There are many different ways to achieve success. Rebecca's story was dramatic, and also incredibly unusual in the huge rewards and risks that it brought her. But no matter the level of the success, any form of external validation can have an addictive quality. Like a drug, getting praise or attention gives you an intense but short-lived rush and often leaves you feeling empty and craving more. Or like the Subtraction Stew in the children's novel *The Phantom Tollbooth* that makes you hungrier the more you eat, achievements can lead to a greater desire for more, "better" achievements, a sense of the stakes being raised with each new accomplishment—and of you perennially falling short. No matter how grand the scale of your success, there's always some way you could have done even better, or someone else to envy.

As my grandfather used to say when my mother or one of her siblings brought home an A minus on a report card: "So, why the minus?"

This carousel never stops—and you can see yourself as stuck on it, riding your wooden pony in circles without ever getting anywhere.

Or you can see that horse you're riding as alive and part of how your journey continually makes you a wiser, stronger human. Horse behaviorist Jenni Purcell describes the process of learning horsemanship as "a quest of never-ending self-improvement." Training a horse, like being a writer, provides a limitless supply of benchmarks by which to measure yourself. With innumerable possible goals to achieve, you will never have a reason to stop challenging yourself, to stop growing. You are never "done" as a writer.

You are never "done" as a writer.

Let your Steed guide you, always, back to craft, back to refining your process, back to the mission that first began your creative journey. When you allow all that to be at the center of your actions, you can let the highs of external validation and lows of rejection buffet you and fall away. The highs that come from your personal successes—the kind you've been achieving as you've worked your way through this book—are deeper, longer-lasting, and can propel you through any lows that the journey brings.

EXERCISE: RIDING THE STEED INTO BATTLE

This exercise shows you how to use your Steed to help you process reactions, both positive and negative, to your work.

the hero is you

1. IDENTIFY THE SOURCE

   From whom did this response come? Rate how highly you value this person's opinion on a scale of one to ten, one being "not at all" and ten being "more highly than anyone else's in the world."

2. POLARIZE THE REACTION

   If the person's comments were more complex than a simple "yes" or "no," divide them into two categories, complimentary and critical. What is generous or affirming in the compliments? What is constructive in the criticism? Do you agree with either? Both? Some but not all?

3. GET ON YOUR PONY

   Take a step back from the response. Imagine this was written about somebody else's work. Viewing it as objectively as you can, how would you characterize it? Insightful? Careless? Sycophantic? What does its tone tell you about how seriously you want to take it?

4. CHECK YOUR MOTIVATIONS

   If you did the previous exercise, you got a chance to consider your expectations before sending out your work. Now that you've gotten a response to it, go back to those motivations. What did you hope would happen with the piece? What did you fear would happen? Has either come to pass? What has happened and what does it feel like?

5. ACTION

   Do you want to extract any feedback from the reaction and apply it to your work? Do you want to rip the response up into tiny pieces and flush them down the toilet? Do you want to call an Ally and commiserate? How do you want what you are experiencing right now to inform your actions in the future?

The "F" Word

There are many ways to define and achieve success—but what about failure?

J. Holtham decided in college that he wanted to be a playwright. All his friends were theater majors, but he didn't act, so as a way to spend more time having fun with them, he started writing plays. After graduation, he moved to New York City and discovered he had both a talent for it and a nonstop stream of ideas, and for the next decade, he was a prolific writer, penning nearly one full-length play each year and dozens of short works for festivals and commissions.

His plays got readings all over New York. They nearly always received enthusiastic responses from audiences and detailed notes from the companies mounting the readings. J. would address the notes and resubmit the plays. But it always stopped there. Despite all this activity, his work just wasn't getting full productions.

Then, in 2006, he was tapped for an incredible opportunity. He was among ten playwrights of color commissioned by Second Stage, one of the most prestigious Off-Broadway companies, to each create a new play. The other writers selected included Pulitzer Prize winners and some of the top playwrights in the field, and J. was honored to be in their company. It was made clear that this commission was geared, ultimately, toward production.

J. wrote what he felt was one of the best plays of his career, and perfect for Second Stage's audience. It was very different from his past work, a deeply personal show about his childhood, featuring a small cast and a minimal set. J. pushed all his own boundaries as a writer, challenging himself to do work that went beyond anything he'd done before. When Second Stage gave him notes, he attacked the rewrites with zeal, determined to take this one all the way.

It was the week before Christmas in 2008 and J. was walking from his day-job office to the subway, past the glittering lights and dressed-up shop windows of midtown, when he got the call from Second Stage. They were not going forward with his play. It was over.

"I was just broken," J. told me.

He said that period of his life makes him think of a line from the TV series *Justified*: "You run into an asshole in the morning, you ran into an asshole; you run into assholes all day, you're the asshole." After this

the hero is you

particularly devastating rejection landed on the pile, J. began to seriously wonder if he was, in fact, the asshole.

"We build a lot of structures around ourselves to protect us from that truth," J. said, "but the fact is, some people just write shitty plays— or plays that are good, but aren't good enough. None of the techniques that I'd learned or knew how to use were making my plays any better. I thought, *I can't keep putting myself through this, working on a play for months or years and it's still not good enough.*"

So, in 2015, J. officially quit playwriting.

But he didn't quit writing. He packed his bags, moved to Los Angeles, and became a screenwriter. J. found that his particular style was a better fit for television and film, and in that world, he saw clear, reachable benchmarks to improve his work and help advance his career.

After years of striving, he'd had to face the hard truth that it was possible the problem was his work. But that didn't mean he had to throw away everything he'd done and learned. It meant initiating a reinvention—finding a new way to be a writer and seeking success with different goals.

J. acknowledged that his work may have been the source of his "failure" as a playwright, but he understood that didn't mean *he* was a failure. Although he had many dark nights of the soul during the process, he didn't come out of it with a Shadow stopping him from writing entirely. He considered quitting and going back to school to study human resources or psychotherapy, but in the end, he knew he was a writer and that he needed to keep writing. He just needed a new set of realistic goals to work toward.

Ultimately, people's judgments on your work—whether they love it or hate it—are not about *you.* And that's a good thing, because your work has infinite capacity to evolve, change, grow, even take a different form like J.'s did. No matter what your work looks like today, it can always get better tomorrow.

No matter what your work looks like today, it can always get better tomorrow.

Discussing failure in his book *Emotional First Aid*, psychologist Guy Winch suggests a number of techniques to turn failure into a constructive experience. The advice is so good, I'm tempted to repeat it all verbatim, but what all his suggestions share is an encouragement toward a shift in perspective. Developing a healthy sense of perspective can help you see, for example, the ways in which every past failure taught you something that led you to ultimate success, opened you up to new opportunities, or made your next achievement more meaningful.

In the span of decades, what we deem our "successes" and "failures" wind up being less important than how we have lived our lives. Winch quotes studies proving that "steady progress toward our goals contributes more toward our sustained happiness and self-fulfillment than actually reaching them." Continuing to pursue a passion that drives us and pushes us to write better, find a more effective process, and evolve as individuals is the true measure of our success.

In other words, regardless of how others respond to you or your work, the journey really is the destination—for the rest of your life.

> *Continuing to pursue a passion that drives us and pushes us to write better, find a more effective process, and evolve as individuals is the true measure of our success.*

the hero is you

mentor-hero

be a mentor for the next hero's journey

After completing her MFA in creative writing, Susan Shapiro missed the camaraderie and feedback she'd gotten from participating in regular workshops. So she decided to start her own writers' group, made up of people she'd met while getting her master's degree at New York University and working at the *New Yorker*. She recruited, in her words, "whoever I thought was smarter than I was," bribed them with popcorn and cheap wine, and invited them to her apartment one night a week.

She told me she didn't see herself as playing a Mentor role in the group, as many of the participants were older and more experienced in the literary world than she was. But "somebody had to run it," so she emulated the way her favorite writing professors at NYU—E.L. Doctorow, Joseph Brodsky, Galway Kinnell—had run their classes.

The meetings began at seven-thirty and initially went until around eleven in the evening. Soon, though, they were stretching until three in the morning. All those smart people didn't want to leave.

Shapiro's group ended up running for eighteen years and producing hundreds of published books, articles, and plays. It led to Susan becoming a professor at the New School in 1993. More than two decades later, she still teaches there. Eighty-five of her former students have published books.

In the middle, she became a bestselling author herself. She has published ten books, including *Only as Good as Your Word: Writing Lessons From My Favorite Literary Gurus,* and hundreds of articles in national newspapers and magazines. And she is still writing.

After enough years of practicing the Hero's Journey of the writing process, Susan Shapiro became a **Mentor-Hero**: someone who could guide others through their journeys while continuing to learn, change, and grow in her own.

At the end of the Hero's Journey he or she becomes, in Campbell's words, the "Master of Two Worlds"—a person with the capacity to understand that the apparent opposites of home and the magical world can coexist. No longer afraid of death and the other terrors embodied by the Shadow, the Hero is now able to live a fully present life.

As Maureen Murdock wrote, "She no longer needs to blame the other; she *is* the other." The opposition between the Hero and Shadow ultimately becomes irrelevant as the Hero recognizes that they are two sides of the same coin. With this powerful knowledge, the Hero is able to become a Mentor to the next Hero on his or her own quest for identity and wholeness.

The writer's journey never truly ends—the need to write is a lifelong compulsion.

The writer's journey never truly ends—the need to write is a lifelong compulsion. But as you wrap up your process on the project you've been focusing on throughout this book and take a moment to reflect on everything you've learned, allow this milestone to be an ending of one kind—and a beginning of another.

EXERCISE: LOOKING BACK ON THE JOURNEY

This exercise crystallizes what you've learned on your journey through the writing process. For each chapter, list one to three boons—the lessons, experiences, surprises—that you most appreciated or that you think you'll use most in your writing process in the future.

HERO: You became a Hero.

You identified whom you most admire, recognized yourself as a hero and your process and life as a journey, clarified your motivation and goals, and explored your source of vulnerability.

The boons I gained were . . .

HERALD: The Herald called you to adventure.

You saw how inspiration can come from anywhere, learned tools to jumpstart it, addressed reluctance to begin a project, clarified the nature of the project you want to start, and looked at how to create change in your life.

The boons I gained were . . .

ALLIES: You marshaled your Allies to join you.

You acknowledged the importance of having a support system, identified who forms this system in your life, and took note of who can provide you with understanding, accountability, and honesty.

The boons I gained were . . .

MENTOR: A wise Mentor gave you guidance.

You worked on listening to your inner wisdom by personifying it, gathered the qualities of your favorite teachers to apply to yourself, stayed grounded about gurus, built structure into your process, and let your intuition guide you toward healthy decisions and show you how to learn from your experiences.

The boons I gained were . . .

THRESHOLD GUARDIANS: You reached the threshold to the magical world and overcame its guardians.

You identified what kind of distraction you're most susceptible to and why, investigated the source of that distraction, explored techniques for neutralizing it to get into a flow state, and looked at how these predilections affect your life outside of writing.

The boons I gained were . . .

SHAPESHIFTER: You met a Shapeshifter and learned how to become one.

You looked at your work and your life through the eyes of your Opposite or a stranger, created a personal mythology to identify the variety of your needs and the tools to address them during your process, and recognized how seeing the world as a writer can give you a new perspective on experiences while benefiting your work.

The boons I gained were . . .

TRICKSTER: You encountered a Trickster and found the Trickster in yourself.

You released yourself from your expectations about what or how you "should" be writing, embraced the value of humor, took a break from the structures you created, and recaptured a sense of fun and play.

The boons I gained were . . .

GODDESS: You fell in love in the heart of nature and participated in creation.

You recognized the inherent cycles in the writing process, pinpointed which you enjoy and which you struggle with most, assessed your natural rhythm and way of working, and witnessed that life's larger cycles can benefit your writing even when they take you away from it.

The boons I gained were . . .

SHADOW: You faced the greatest source of darkness in the magical world.

You identified what stops you from writing, investigated its origins, developed a range of tools to address it faced it head-on, saw how your struggle can lead to a breakthrough in your writing, and took a fresh look at your goals and what you're capable of.

The boons I gained were . . .

SUPERHERO: You were reborn as a greater version of yourself and embarked on the journey back.

You channeled your past experiences to help you complete your project, identified and addressed obstacles to finishing, celebrated the milestone of reaching the end of your draft, inventoried your tools and developed new ones to help you revise your work, and observed how what you learn from revising your writing can help you revise your view of yourself and your life.

The boons I gained were . . .

STEED: You rode your trusty mount all the way home to share what you learned with your people.

You figured out how to tell when you're ready to ask for feedback, set your intentions to better handle constructive criticism, encouraged yourself to absorb compliments, used your intuition to decide what advice to take and what to ignore, clarified your motivations before sending out your work for professional consideration, found a wellspring of validation in yourself, let craft keep you focused, found healthy ways to process people's responses to your work, and maintained perspective.

The boons I gained were . . .

What you've accomplished deserves celebrating. Even if you didn't read the book and do each exercise straight through, if you've reached this point, take time to acknowledge what you have done. The journey is not a one-and-done experience, so you may return to this book again in the future and do the exercises or glean the lessons that didn't make it into this particular iteration of your process.

You have achieved a tremendous series of feats, and now you are at a remarkable milestone. The work you have done has made you stronger, more courageous, and more resilient. Think about the skills you rated yourself on in the first chapter—how have you improved each one? Think about the way you first viewed yourself as a Hero. Who is the Hero turned Superhero turned Hero-Mentor who now looks back at you in the mirror?

Words of Mentors

As you've seen, there is much more to take away from the writing process than a finished piece of work and whatever external recognition it might bring you. Completing this project has been a tremendous accomplishment—and whenever you are ready, it's time to do it again, and again after that. Each piece you write is a vehicle for you to sharpen your skills and hone your process in this never-ending spiral. You will repeat the Hero's Journey over and over and over. And each time, you'll be a better writer with healthier habits and a life that is more fully integrated with your work.

> *Each piece you write is a vehicle for you to sharpen your skills and hone your process in this never-ending spiral.*

Don't take it from me, though. Here's what a few of the writers you've gotten to know have said about this:

"Every book feels like a miracle. It's the one profession that feels like it never gets easier, because every book is so different and so hard in its own way. Surgeons, the more surgery they do, they must get better at it, feel more comfortable every time they walk into the operating room. Whereas when I'm sitting down to that first page, sometimes I feel just as insecure as I did the very first time."—Stefanie Pintoff

"The more I'm reviewed and the more plays I write, the less it becomes about one play or one review. If there's anything I'm starting to learn—and I've still got a lot more to learn—it's that it's about a body of work. . . . It's about all these plays and how they connect and how they're in conversation with each other."—Sam Hunter

"I feel like a kindergartener with every project that I start."—Cari Lynn

"You'd think it would be less painful at the beginning, but every book starts with the same self-doubt, confusion, feeling overwhelmed by the number of choices, and every time I just somehow get through it and have to recognize that I have a process—it's not the most fun process, but it's a process. And the more you write, the more you accept your own process, through experience."—MacKenzie Cadenhead

"Every time you complete a project, the next one is always starting to sprout, and you always have to go back to zero and do everything all over again. Even in therapy, I go back and I'm like, 'I thought I already dealt with these issues—I already wrote about this!'"—Kyoung Park

"With childbirth, I've heard a lot of the time your body doesn't remember how badly it hurts, so you'll do it again—which is pretty dickish of your body. I think that's a factor in performing and in living and experiencing life—giving birth to your ideas and having them crushed. It's not for the faint of heart: being a writer, being an artist, putting your work out there, having people criticize it . . . but at the same time if you can handle it, the rewards are really wonderful."
—Jessica Delfino

"When this is no longer a challenge, I'll quit . . . I don't write for anyone else; I'm not writing for an audience. I'm writing because I have to. I don't go to the gym. I probably should go to the gym. I've gone to the gym in my life and it makes me feel much better and it quells my anxiety, but so does writing. Writing is my gym. When you love something, you want to be the best at it, and to be the best at it, you have to figure out ways to devote your days to it that are productive."
—Amanda Stern

"The nice thing is, there's always the next project—so if you really think you missed something, pick it up in the next project. I get bored—I do the project, I pour my soul into it, it makes me insane, and then at a certain point I just can't look at it anymore."—Negin Farsad

"Each book is its own creature, and you have to treat it as its own thing. My first book is like the kid I had too young, and as I look back on the more than a decade it took to get to publication, I can see in it every mistake I ever made, the hard lessons that that book and I learned together."—Brian Herrera

---

This thrilling moment, the end of this journey, is also just one dot on a timeline that forms a whole life as a writer.

You may find that everything you've learned while working through this book gets turned topsy-turvy when you try to apply it to your next project. Each new piece will take you through a different

This thrilling moment, the end of this journey, is also just one dot on a timeline that forms a whole life as a writer.

process with different experiences and new lessons to learn. The journey cannot be relied upon for consistency; it will always surprise and challenge you.

Let's look at how to integrate everything you've learned so you can continue to use these tools after you finish reading this book.

EXERCISE: LOOKING FORWARD

It's easier to stick to healthy habits, ways of thinking, and practices when you have the structure of the book to follow. You are welcome to use this book to help you through the process of as many projects as you wish, but you'll never again read it for the first time. This exercise will help you move forward with what you've learned on this first adventure.

Divide a page of your journal into three columns.

In the left-most column, create a list of the most common issues you struggle with during the writing process.

In the middle column, write what skill, tool, or idea from this book you would like to use in the future to address this issue.

In the far-right column, write what you'll use to hold you accountable: How will you remind yourself to use this tool? How will you make sure to employ what you've learned?

Post this tri-columned list somewhere you can see it when you're writing.

By Teaching, We Learn

The best way to internalize what you've learned, in any situation, is to teach it to someone else. In fact, a study done at Washington University in St. Louis showed that simply being told you will be expected to teach material to someone else helps you improve the thoroughness, organization, and accuracy of your recall. We are inherently teaching creatures, built on empathy and a desire to share knowledge with others.

Many of the writers you've met in these pages have become teachers and professors who pass on what they've learned to less experienced students of the craft. Others are more informal Mentors to younger writers who've sought them out. Some simply share what they've learned with the Allies who have become their partners in evolution.

At the beginning of our journey together, I challenged you to see yourself as a Hero; now, I challenge you to see yourself as Mentor-Hero, adding to your mission the mandate of helping others navigate the road of the writing process.

For me, the opportunity to use everything I had learned as a coach, editor, and teacher—and through my own difficulties with the writing process—was what brought me back to writing after a long separation. The more I saw writers walk away from my workshops, coaching sessions, speeches, and conversations feeling inspired, the more inspired I felt. The more I heard myself asking them questions, giving them feedback, and encouraging them to heed their inner wisdom, the more I felt able to take my own advice. The joy of helping other writers spurred me to complete my first major writing project in over a decade—this book.

The Hero's Journey of the writing process, for me, became about much more than just writing. I suspect that will be the case for you, too.

Catharsis

While you have been creating a finished piece of writing and developing a more constructive process, you have also been hard at work on another, deeper agenda: discovering how to live a more satisfying, more connected, happier life and letting go of old habits, insecurities, and fears that have held you back.

The ancient Greeks didn't attend plays for sheer entertainment. They went to the theater to experience the full range of human emotions and, through the characters they witnessed onstage, purge themselves of the feelings they wanted to expunge, like pity and fear. When they pitied Oedipus for his fate and feared being ravaged by loss like Antigone, they released those emotions so they could return to their lives feeling freer, with less weighing on their own hearts. They called this cleansing *kátharsis*.

To this day, we apply this to Western storytelling: we must see the Hero experience some form of catharsis at the end of his journey, or the story's arc will not feel complete and the audience will not be able to walk away with the sense that something has been opened up within them.

Stories don't have this effect only on their audiences—they are also cathartic for their creators. Writing gives us the opportunity to understand our emotions and explain our lives to ourselves. Every challenge you've worked through in developing your writing process has given you tools to use in the challenges you face out there in the world: dealing with obstacles to your desires, making tough decisions, overcoming trauma.

> *Writing gives us the opportunity to understand our emotions and explain our lives to ourselves.*

Each time we experience the catharsis of the writing process, we become better equipped to help others reach their own catharsis, through their enjoyment of our writing and through creating their own. This is also what it means to be a Mentor-Hero: to enhance not only your life, but the lives of others around you. To see that we are all Heroes on journeys—seeking to know who we are, why we're here, and how to do the hard work of living.

In *The Power of Myth*, Campbell calls artists contemporary shamans "whose ears are open to the song of the universe." Maureen Murdock says that when the Heroine returns from her journey with all she's learned, "she brings that wisdom back to share with the world. And the women, men, and children of the world are transformed by her journey."

Writers make the myths that become the language of culture, the lens through which people look at their world and at themselves. Without writers, there would be no journey, no archetypes, no catharsis. Without writers, humans would lack the tools to understand themselves and one another. Your job is among the most important on the entire planet: spinning the web of myth that holds the world up, that weaves our psyches together.

You are a Hero. You have the power to change minds, move hearts, and deliver wisdom to your fellow human beings. Writing is hard. It's always going to be. But every step of the journey you take allows you to create transformation in the lives of others, and to lessen the separation between *them* and *us*, between *me* and *you*.

Says Campbell: "People have the notion of saving the world by shifting things around, changing the rules, and who's on top, and so forth. No, no! Any world is a valid world if it's alive. The thing to do is to bring life to it, and the only way to do that is to find in your own case where the life is and become alive yourself."

Build your world. Bring it to life. Do it again. And trust that what you create will have been well worth the journey.

> *You are a Hero. You have the power to change minds, move hearts, and deliver wisdom to your fellow human beings.*

bibliography

Baze, Alex. Interview by author. Audio recording. New York, August 8, 2015.

Cadenhead, MacKenzie. Interview by author. Audio recording. New York, August 7, 2015.

Cameron, Julia. *The Artist's Way*. New York: Jeremy P. Tarcher, 1992.

Campbell, Joseph. *The Hero with a Thousand Faces*. Princeton: Princeton University Press, 1949.

Campbell, Joseph (with Moyers, Bill). *The Power of Myth*. New York: Bantam Dell Doubleday Publishing Group, Inc., 1988.

"Christmas Season Marked by Obscenities." Catholic League website. Retrieved from catholicleague.org.

Csikszentmihalyi, Mihaly. *Flow: The Psychology of Optimal Experience*. New York: Harper and Row, 1990.

Currey, Mason. *Daily Rituals: How Artists Work*. New York: Alfred A. Knopf, 2013.

Delfino, Jessica. Interview by author. Audio recording. New York, June 26, 2015.

Everding, Gerry. "Students Learn More if They'll Need to Teach Others." Web blog post. *Futurity*. August 12, 2014. Web. July 15, 2015.

Fadiman, Anne. Interview by author. Email. New York, October 4, 2015.

Farsad, Negin. Interview by author. Audio recording. New York, July 9, 2015.

Flaherty, Alice W. *The Midnight Disease: The Drive to Write, Writer's Block, and the Creative Brain*. New York: Houghton Mifflin Company, 2004.

Gaiman, Neil. Website of Neil Gaiman. Retrieved from *neilgaiman.com*.

Goleman, Daniel. *Focus: The Hidden Driver of Excellence*. New York: HarperCollins Publishers, 2013.

Gottschall, Jonathan. *The Storytelling Animal: How Stories Make Us Human*. New York: Houghton Mifflin Harcourt, 2012.

Hadhazy, Adam. "Think Twice: How the Gut's 'Second Brain' Influences Mood and Well-Being." Web blog post. *Scientific American*. Nature America, Inc., Feb. 12, 2010. Web. July 18, 2015.

Herrera, Brian. Interview by author. Audio recording. New York, July 8, 2015.

Holtham, J. Interview by author. Audio recording. New York, June 17, 2015.

Hunter, Sam. Interview by author. Audio recording. New York, June 12, 2015.

Hurwitz, Mitchell. "NYTVF's 2013 Creative Keynote: Mitchell Hurwitz." Keynote speech, New York Television Festival, New York City, October 13, 2015.

"I Was the Voice of Democracy." *Theatre from the Land of Enchantment*. The Public Radio Exchange. Cambridge, MA: PRX. June 1, 2011.

Jackman, Ian. *The Writer's Mentor*. New York: Random House Reference, 2004.

Jackson, Michael R. Interview by author. Audio recording. New York, July 1, 2015.

Johnson, Celia Blue. *Odd Type Writers*. New York: Perigee, 2013.

Justified. "Hole in the Wall." Season 4, Episode 1. Directed by Michael Dinner. Written by Graham Yost and Elmore Leonard. FX, January 8, 2013.

Kaplan, Myq. Interview by author. Audio recording. New York, July 6, 2015.

Kottler, Jeffrey A. *Change: What* Really *Leads to Lasting Personal Transformation*. New York: Oxford University Press, 2014.

Lamott, Anne. *Bird By Bird*. New York: Doubleday, 1994.

Lynn, Cari. Interview by author. Audio recording. New York, September 9, 015

McKee, Ruth. Interview by author. Audio recording. New York, July 27, 2015.

Moody, Rick. Interview by author. Email. New York, May 24, 2015.

Murdock, Maureen. *The Heroine's Journey*. Boston: Shambhala Press, 1990.

Nye, Bill. Commencement speech, Rutgers University Commencement, New Brunswick, New Jersey, May 17, 2015.

Ortberg, Mallory. Interview by author. Audio recording. New York, August 26, 2015.

Park, Kyoung. Interview by author. Audio recording. New York, June 8, 2015.

Pennebaker, James W. Website of James W. Pennebaker. Retrieved from homepage.psy.utexas.edu/homepage/faculty/pennebaker/home2000/jwphome.htm.

Pierson, DC. Interview by author. Audio recording. New York, July 12, 2015.

Pintoff, Stefanie. Interview by author. Audio recording. New York, August 26, 2015.

Purcell, Jenni. Interview by author. Email. New York, April 3, 2016.

Ramachandran, V.S. *A Brief Tour of Human Consciousness*. London: Pi Press, 2004.

Rilke, Rainer Maria. *Letters to a Young Poet*. Mitchell, Stephen, translation. Boston: Shambhala Press, 1984.

Sandberg, Sheryl. *Lean In*. New York: Alfred A. Knopf, 2013.

Saunders, George. Interview by author. Audio recording. New York, June 22, 2015.

Sethi, Mehar. Interview by author. Audio recording. New York, August 31, 2015.

Shapiro, Susan. Interview by author. Audio recording. New York, July 18, 2015.

Steel, Sharon. Interview by author. Audio recording. New York, July 22, 2015.

Stern, Amanda. Interview by author. Audio recording. New York, August 3, 2015.

Tugend, Alina. "Praise is Fleeting, But Brickbats We Recall." Web blog post. *Your Money*. *The New York Times*, March 23, 2012. Web. August 3, 2015.

Vogler, Christopher. *The Writer's Journey* (Second Edition). Studio City, CA: Michael Wiese Productions, 1998.

Vonnegut, Kurt. *Palm Sunday: An Autobiographical Collage*. New York: Dial Press, 1999.

Wade, Adam. Interview by author. Audio recording. New York, June 17, 2015.

Website of Wizards of the Coast. Retrieved from wizards.com.

Weems, Scott. *Ha!: The Science of When We Laugh and Why*. New York: Basic Books, 2014.

Wilson, Timothy D. *Redirect: Changing the Stories We Live By.* New York: Little Brown, 2011.

Winch, Guy. *Emotional First Aid: Practical Strategies for Treating Failure, Rejection, Guilt, and Other Everyday Psychological Injuries.* New York: Hudson Street Press, 2013.

Wiseman, Richard. *59 Seconds: Change Your Life in Under a Minute.* New York: Anchor Books, 2010.

"Why Saying Is Believing—The Science of Self-Talk." Narrated by Laura Starecheski. Morning Edition. *NPR*, October 7, 2014. npr.org/sections/health-shots/2014/10/07/353292408/why-saying-is-believing-the-science-of-self-talk.

Yahoo! News website. Retrieved from news.yahoo.com.

Younge, Gary. "Bayard Rustin: The Gay Black Pacifist at the Heart of the March on Washington." Web blog post. *The Guardian.* August 23, 2013. Web. April 1, 2016.

acknowledgments

The process of turning these ideas into *The Hero Is You* has been an exercise in taking (or, more often, struggling to take) my own advice. The irony was not lost on me that every time I had trouble finding focus, curbing my perfectionism, or maintaining a sense of play there was a chapter to treat that ailment in my own book, if only I could manage to write the damn thing. My boundless gratitude is due to those who helped me, in all the ways I couldn't help myself, on this book's journey from idea to publication.

My huge thanks go out to the whole team at Red Wheel/Weiser. I'm so grateful to my editor Caroline Pincus: thank you for having a vision for this project and offering your graceful and wise input. Publisher Michael Kerber, you have been a patient and generous partner in the process of bringing this book into the world. My thanks, also, to the wonderful marketing team and sales group at Red Wheel/Weiser for your hard work in getting *The Hero Is You* into people's hands.

It's quite an experience to see your thoughts morph from a Word document into an object you can hold. For that, I'm enormously grateful to designer Cara Petrus for her gorgeous cover and to Jim Hoover for providing the spot art and diagrams. Thanks, also, to Debby Dutton, the interior designer, for pulling it all together; to Ashley Benning, the copyeditor, for your eagle eye; and to production editor Jane Hagaman for facilitating the entire process.

Writing this book was a wonderful excuse to spend a whole summer getting to ask a varied and talented group of writers all kinds of questions and pick their extraordinary brains. My thanks are due to all the writers willing to contribute their time to be interviewed for the book: Alex Baze, MacKenzie Cadenhead, Jessica Delfino, Anne Fadiman, Negin Farsad, Brian Herrera, J. Holtham, Sam Hunter, Michael R. Jackson, Lexie Kahanovitz, Myq Kaplan, Cari Lynn, Ruth McKee, Rick Moody, Mallory Ortberg, Kyoung Park, DC Pierson, Stefanie Pintoff, Leila Sales, George Saunders, Rebecca Serle, Mehar Sethi, Susan Shapiro, Sharon Steel, Amanda Stern, and Adam Wade. Please check out their books, TV shows, plays, articles, blogs, stand-up, and other creations. Follow them on social media. Support talented artists who are also kind and generous people!

Tremendous thanks are also due to my coaching clients who allowed me to share their stories here. Their names and identifying details have been changed, and some are composites, but all the experiences described are drawn from the inventive, driven, and courageous people who inspire me and keep me completely in love with being a coach. I'm also grateful to the Society of Children's Book Writers and Illustrators community and to my students, past and present, from Mediabistro, the Bard Prison Initiative, and the Focus Forward Project.

In addition to my clients, another brilliant group of writers beta-tested the exercises in this book and offered their generous feedback to help me improve the material. Thank you so much to Jennifer Baker, Lynn Becker, Billy Merrell, Sara Ortiz, Anica Rissi, Leila Sales, Kerry Sparks, and Kyoung Park for your honesty and insight.

I wrote *The Hero Is You* while working full-time as an editor at Penguin (and coaching and teaching!). I owe a tremendous debt of gratitude to those who—consciously or not—provided spaces where I could retreat and focus on my passion project on weekends and vacations.

Thank you to the DiCampo family, Pamela Perrell, Patricia Finn, and the proprietors and baristas of Cocoa Bar in Brooklyn and Madiba in Harlem for the peace, refuge, and chai lattes.

The studies of Joseph Campbell have given us so many beautiful ways to talk about story and storytelling. I offer much reverence and respect to him and to the other scholars and authors whose work inspired and informed *The Hero Is You.*

I've said much about the importance of Allies and feel rich beyond measure to have incredible friends who have been my twins, my witnesses, my soothsayers, and so much more. I might never have stopped noodling and started pursuing publication without the encouragement of Anica Rissi and help from Kerry Sparks. My gratitude also goes to Kate Trainor, Rebecca Serle, and Joe Quinones for their support and advice in navigating the road to publication. Thank you to Tony Flynt, Lexie Kahanovitz, Jennifer Baker, Kisha Edwards, and my other artist friends who continually amaze me with your strength and resilience in your own creative journeys.

My thanks go especially to three people I can't imagine living without. Joy Peskin, you are the most empathetic, wise, funny, generous Mentor anyone could ever ask for, and your boundless support for me, in this project and in all my endeavors, buoys my confidence and has shaped who I am today. Leila Sales, another incredibly generous person who shares so much more with me than can fit in any Venn diagram, if I tried to write down all the ways you have been there for me, it would fill another whole book. Everyone should be lucky enough to have a friend like you. Joel Putnam, patient preserver of my sanity, perpetual elevator of my mood, and a true Hero who makes the world a better place every day, especially my world, your faith in me makes me feel weak at the knees and strong in the heart. Thank you for helping me finish this most challenging of sandwiches.

Gratitude forever to my parents, Rita and Larry Levin. You raised me to love and respect creativity and artistic expression, and you've always encouraged me to listen to my passions and follow them wherever they might lead. If everyone had parents who treated them with as much love as you've given me, this world would be a very different, and much happier, place.

Lastly, there are two people without whom this book simply wouldn't exist:

Lindsay Edgecombe, agent nonpareil, you saw the potential in my very rough proposal and took a year of your time to help me craft an abstract project into something much tighter and more focused. You found the book a publishing home, then continued to provide invaluable input at every stage of the process. Your fingerprints are on every page of this book, and it's so much better for it. You've been a tireless advocate, consummate strategist, and trusted advisor. I can't thank you enough, though I will probably keep trying.

Andrea Adams, my former babysitter, onetime camp counselor, and always friend, I'd been daydreaming of creating an advice book for writers for years until our conversation sparked this idea. You shared your own studies on the Hero's Journey with me, lent me your books, and spent countless hours talking ideas and letting me bounce my thoughts off you. You helped me hold on to this project until I finally had the confidence to carry it with both hands. You have been, and will always be, an inextricable part of this book and the ideas it contains. Thank you.

the hero is you

about the author

Photo © Allison Stock

Kendra Levin is a certified life coach for writers, as well as an editor, teacher, and award-winning writer. Since 2008, she has helped creative artists meet their goals and connect more deeply with their work and themselves. She has been an editor at Penguin for over a decade. Kendra has taught classes to everyone from media professionals to prison inmates and her eclectic professional writing credits include celebrity speeches, bar guides, and Mad Libs. Visit her at *kendracoaching.com* and follow her @kendralevin.

to our readers

Conari Press, an imprint of Red Wheel/Weiser, publishes books on topics ranging from spirituality, personal growth, and relationships to women's issues, parenting, and social issues. Our mission is to publish quality books that will make a difference in people's lives—how we feel about ourselves and how we relate to one another. We value integrity, compassion, and receptivity, both in the books we publish and in the way we do business.

Our readers are our most important resource, and we appreciate your input, suggestions, and ideas about what you would like to see published.

Visit our website at *www.redwheelweiser.com* to learn about our upcoming books and free downloads, and be sure to go to *www.red wheelweiser.com/newsletter* to sign up for newsletters and exclusive offers.

You can also contact us at *info@rwwbooks.com*.

Conari Press
an imprint of Red Wheel/Weiser, LLC
65 Parker Street, Suite 7
Newburyport, MA 01950
www.redwheelweiser.com